The Odyssey of a Heart
innocence, drugs, and the pursuit of Freedom

Mervin Wagler

Copyright © 2007 by Mervin Wagler

The Odyssey of a Heart
innocence, drugs, and the pursuit of Freedom
by Mervin Wagler

Printed in the United States of America

ISBN 978-1-60266-274-2

All rights reserved solely by the author. The author guarantees all contents are original and do not infringe upon the legal rights of any other person or work. No part of this book may be reproduced in any form without the permission of the author. The views expressed in this book are not necessarily those of the publisher.

www.xulonpress.com

to my five brothers
    John
        David
            Reuben
            Glen
                Samuel
                    words could never tell
                    how much you mean to me

Chapter One

The growl of the engine in my '84 Iroc Z pulses in my brain as I drive east through the northeast Missouri darkness. The road disappears steadily underneath the hood as I lean back in the comfortable seat, left hand resting easy on the steering wheel. My head is light, my nose numb, my whole body gripped in a bone jarring rush. I am on top of the world; high as a kite, loaded with drugs, the open road before. The engine shifts down and the roar of the straight pipes becomes a living thing as I pick up speed.

Earlier I stopped by my supplier's house in anticipation of the weekend ahead, now I'm heading out of state for a few days to visit friends and to party, to get wasted on some good dope. Thankfully I have good access to a variety of drugs that feeds my insatiable appetite for the same. After snorting a line of crank and smoking some, I hit the road. With me are a few joints, an ounce of weed, and several grams of meth. The danger of my illegal activities probes the back recesses of my mind, however, fear is not alive.

The Odyssey of a Heart

Settling into the seat, I take stock of my surroundings. The world that rests in the penetrating gaze of the headlights lies in crystal clear observance. A warm relaxed feeling creeps silently into my chest as the drugs grip more firmly onto my mind and body. The lonely, painful strains of Kurt Cobain's guitar drift from the Rockford Fosgate speakers and the subs pound away in the back. No past exists, equally no future. Only the present is alive. The only place in the world is inside my car. Just me and the open road.

This place of chemical solitude I love almost better than life itself. This lonely yet fulfilling plane serves me all I need. My body feels great. My mind floats. Reality gels me into the outside elements of the road, my car, and the surrounding nature. In this world of the immediate moment, I reign as king and lord of all.

Striking a balance opposite my detached musing, the rapidly moving road keeps me zoned in. Been only a time or two I forgot I was in a hurtling chunk of iron in complete dependence on me for safety. Not so now. The old Missouri hills keep the tempo rolling as up and down we go. A 45 mph limit begins and I conscientiously slow down and cruise into Wayland. Time to head 'er south. State road 61 is just ahead; my left hand glides forward and hits the turn signal up. Click, click, click. Sweeping around the curve, I put a little pressure on the gas and the engine roars. Past a scant few houses and I'm out of town.

The road lies on hills and long curves. No one else is out tonight. I've met but a car or two in the better part of an hour. Neither of these was a cop. I'd love to punch the gas and hit the road in a powerful burst of speed my car is so capable of. But I don't. No point in being stupid. A small cliff rises to my right. On the left, fields drop slowly away for a few miles only to sink in subjugation to the mighty Mississippi. I am in communion with the road that carries me, slicing through the unknown darkness. It does not worry itself with the world at large. It only winds through the night, steeling its shoulders to support the occasional passer.

I have always loved the open road, long thrilling to the possibilities of routes to be traveled and places to be seen. Clearly I remember driving these very hills and curves years ago, seated on the edge of the back seat in a fourteen passenger van as our family journeyed to Ohio. Taking trips was big stuff.

We couldn't just jump in and go, however. Our Amish religion forbade ownership of automobiles, so we'd hire an "Amish taxi" to transport us the hundred, five hundred, or thousand miles we needed to go. The rest of the time, the horse and buggy combination transported us to where we needed to be, albeit slowly.

Roads, bridges, rivers, towns. I remember much of the travels of my youth. Now I am in my element. I smoke my joint, laced with the powder. I float over the countryside. Here I feel at home, here on the road. Nothing bothers me. There exists neither good nor evil. I am alone.

I am separated from my past, with its myriad thrills and joys, warmth and security; with its forces of anger and fear, coldness and doubt. I stare at the highway drifting toward me. The night is dark outside this environment that is my car. This is my world. The earth revolves around me, for I sit with the most important element in my life. I am with my drugs; I am with, indeed I am within, meth. The powder I have smoked and snorted tonight has reached back to my central nervous system and has wrapped her arms tightly around it. This has affected almost all aspects of my present physical and mental experience. The pupils of my eyes stare wide open. Pleasure cells within my brain are released at an increased rate before they race to my body and mind to subdue unpleasant thoughts and feelings. The natural routine of certain cells is interrupted and causes some discomfort anyway. My chest feels hollow and tight, so I light some more weed. I sip water because it feels like the thing to do. And it is, for meth depletes the liquid level of the body.

The road expands to four lanes as I near the roaming grounds of Tom Sawyer and Huck Finn. I draw ever closer to the plain I seek, the capsule of timelessness. Many things I love about meth, but the places it takes my mind I love the best. I love reaching an arena of detachment and desiring to be only there. Time stops; I sit gazing. The road moves toward me- from the right, from the left. My hand moves the steering wheel. It just happens. My head pivots slowly, staring here and there. Each movement lasts an eternity. A guitar swells in my brain. I feel little of body... I drift into this weird night of meth and marijuana. Alone. Alone.

Chapter Two

As a kid I often wondered about my origins. I was surrounded by Grandparents, Aunts, Uncles, and cousins; and at a more intimate level, Parents and siblings. Glorying in the innocence of childhood, I still had a sense of coming from somewhere - from someone.

I can now trace my blood back to Alsace, France in the eighteenth century. One of my forefathers started a long tradition of conservative views by joining himself to the Anabaptist movement; the Christian group characterized by their very literal interpretation of Jesus' teachings. In the mid 1800s four Wagler brothers blazed a path to the new world in search of religious freedom. Farms in Ontario and migration to Indiana moved the stage to the central USA. My ancestors stayed at the front of life as they engaged mind and body in the pursuit of their high ideals, in the pursuit of a godly life. They made their homes in close knit Amish communities, shunning the newest inventions and conveniences, trying to stay set apart from society at large.

My father entered life in 1948 in Daviess county Indiana, the oldest son of David and Ida Mae Wagler. His boyhood speaks of hard work on the farm and excitement in the classroom. Ever the idealist, Grandfather moved to Ohio and then Ontario in search of a balanced environment for the responsibility of raising his children. Here too arrived my mother, Iva Mae Hochstetler, and her family for reasons similar to the above. She had spent her prime childhood years in Shipshewana, Indiana where she was born in 1952, an oldest child.

In 1973 my parents were married in a small school house in rural Honduras. Mother's family had moved there in '71 with the goal of spreading the gospel to the native population, a venture that lasted eight years. The newly weds had other things in mind and spent their first years together all the way back up in Ontario.

My oldest brother and sister, John and Rachel, were born there in Southern Ontario. The faint smog of Detroit tinted the sky as they ran out to greet Father in the evenings, returning from the fields with the ancient dust of labor upon his brow. The fertile soil of the region provided hope for the small farmer my father was. With Mother keeping the home fires burning, life was good.

The late '70s saw another move by most of the Waglers. Seeking out a fresh start in a new location, Grandfather moved his family to Bloomfield, Iowa; a new community with its high ideals still untainted by

The Odyssey of a Heart

the course of time. Great times they had, no doubt. A young, small Christian brotherhood does much to draw its members together.

Two more brothers, David and Reuben, awaited me as I drew my first breath of southeast Iowa air on March 7, 1981. Further, I had three cousins close by, and another cousin entered life a mere two weeks after me. Then there were the numerous aunts and uncles. Family all around. We didn't have far to go for family night at the Grandparents. Our farmstead stood about a quarter mile into the half mile drive leading to the Ole' family farm. Further back in the drive dwelt uncle Titus and his new bride Ruth; with Marvin and aunt Rhoda up on the hill. The main set of buildings sat at the junction of two ridges coming in from the east and the south, with the river bottom spreading out in front. As prime a homestead as southern Iowa has to offer.

Action was nonstop at our house in the early days. With ten children something was always afoot. Five brothers, four sisters, and I lived with our parents on the beautiful land of Southeast Iowa. Our farm consisted of about two hundred acres and provided plenty of hunting and other outdoor activities. The cattle barn housed about fifteen cows that needed to be attended to twice daily. A dozen horses roamed the hills in search of the choicest blades of grass.

John, David, and Reuben blazed a path for me the way older brothers should. Rachel was the big sister that always knew exactly how I *should* be doing things. I had the distinction of being as close to the center of the family as anyone could get. Therefore

I received big sibling influence and was still able to deal some influence to the younger ones; Mary, Glen, Laura, Rosanna, and Samuel rounded out the family.

My earliest memories involve the family seated around the crowded kitchen table, eating salmon soup or the anticipated fried red tomatoes and sweet corn on the cob. The children hollered and argued; the parents desperately guided the daily circus. Later Mother would sweep the dreaded pile of toys, trash, and dirt together and the unlucky ones got to clean up the whole affair. Then there were the gatherings at Grandparents, playing with my best friend Andrew. Grandma's sensational cooking satisfied my taste buds and left on my mind a pleasant mark. Our band of cousins was ever brainstorming innovative ways to spend our time.

My brothers and I roamed the hills as the years ticked by. We played in the creek and hunted blackberries. The ole' threshing machine behind the barn occupied us for hours, and the farm pond served up swimming, fishing, and boating. Our creativity was our only limit.

In my sixth year, the life–altering classroom swung her doors open for me. Lunch box in hand, I walked the two miles to Clearview school as I would do many times in the following eight years. Once there I found knowledge for the mind willing to search it out. The defining moment of the first school year, indeed, of all my school years, came on the day I read in class for the first time. I was growing up!

The Odyssey of a Heart

By the time I'd gotten a few years of school in, John and Rachel had graduated. Now David ran the show and got us to school, sometimes on time. The school wagon was quite a sight. Trusty old Bell pulled the worn out buggy down the road. It sported broken lights and chipped paint alongside the torn skin; the horse had shaggy hair and no bridle. The cheapest traveling circus in town. We even made the front page of the local newspaper. The daily newspaper no less.

Oh, the memories of youth! Your mind rolls back– a picture drifts before your eyes. You recognize it as a scene of an enjoyable event. When was it that we did this? What were we doing? The picture drifts away, now you can't even remember what it was. But it made you *feel* something from the past. You don't know what it is, but it is a memory none the less. Then there are the crystallized scenes that ring their clarion call, bringing back a familiar scene of you and your friends playing (in the creek, perhaps), your family at Christmas, or the face of your second grade teacher. Your childhood keeps giving you a sense of balance and justice. Sure, you got hurt as a child. You have memories from many years ago that still cause you to feel dumb and ashamed, right? Even now! After all these years. But still, above all that prevailed a sense of trust and hope. The world was a good place, with security even. You *trusted* those around you. Your life was as wonderful as you cared to dream. You were happy; you were *secure*. Your joys were basic and easily fueled. A day with your cousins or staying overnight at Grandpa's got

The Odyssey of a Heart

your world jumping with joy. Ah, childhood... And now even a certain smell may trigger something, a pleasant feeling of a day long trodden underfoot by the unstoppable march of time. For just a moment you are a small *innocent* child again and everything is right with your world. Just because you smelled a forgotten scent!

And then... I stood on the threshold of adolescence. To understand my personality of that time, we must first examine some of my inherited traits. I am a Wagler, so I want to adventure; to see, to explore, to do. I constantly desire to experience something new. I am fiercely proud of being a part of the larger Wagler family, the family that is strong and doesn't need help from anyone. Above all, my interests get 100% of my energies. It is the way of Waglers.

For some reason, I developed a distrust of people in general and my Dad in particular as I approached the teens. My strong willed nature and the setting I was in caused me to take my fears and questions inside. I never spoke with an adult about the normal things that bother a growing child, the type of things difficult to reveal. I learned to gain knowledge and make decisions on my own.

Now, I have numerous wonderful memories of growing up. Our family did the things a normal American family does. But as this book will reveal, I was cultivating some very destructive tendencies.

Today's thinking places much emphasis on the child's experience in the home. If he or she grows up and drifts outside the accepted norm for people of a particular setting, blame is immediately placed on some incident or person in his or her past. This can certainly be over emphasized.

Reason tells us that a child's parents have heavy influence on her eventual character as an adult. This rings especially true concerning the father. He is ordained by God to be the representative of God. The child looks to the father as the source for all knowledge and security. In all practical aspects, the child views her father as God himself.

But father lives in a fallen world of sin. He is less than God. Mistakes are inevitable.

No doubt this aspect of life impacted my character development. My dad made mistakes. Is that shocking? Think about your father. Did he ever make mistakes? Did you get hurt by those mistakes? Maybe you are a father. Now you see things from yet another angle.

This situation is the inevitable result of life on earth. All father/ child relationships struggle to some degree. Ours was not a perfect home. However, I think it unnecessary to detail the shortcomings of my loved ones. That being said, there were certain situations that fed my isolating / independent mentality.

I personally know families that have better structure than ours; I know families that are much, much worse. Whatever the case, instead of overcoming the problems of adolescence, I allowed them to harden my heart.

As I chalked up my first teen year, my life was fast becoming complicated. I was changing physically and mentally. My mind reached out, grasping for answers to life's hard questions.

Chapter Three

The pines above us pointed into the sky with gnarled arms and fingers. Several years' accumulation of dead pine needles lay scattered on the ground. The black Iowa dirt managed to peek through only a small portion of the ground surface. The roots were grounded deep with the stability to weather the fiercest storms. On the other side of the row of about fifteen trees, the ground sloped away, but only out of reach of the retaining roots. The trees knew where they stood. They did an honest day's work, performing exactly what their creator prescribed. Firmly entrenched, they peered down on a small group of school aged lads.

One boy held a round can of Skoal tobacco in his right hand. The seal was broken and most of the contents were gone. He had happened to find it, and now several of the boys wanted to try the remains. One lad even boasted of having tasted snuff before.

Reaching into the can, my friend took a pinch and placed it between his lower lip and gum. Two of the others followed suit. The can was held out to me.

I was aware of several facts. First, these actions were forbidden; the secretive atmosphere confirmed this. Plus, I didn't even want to taste tobacco; I didn't particularly like the smell. And I knew my dad wouldn't like it. It was WRONG.

So what did I do? "I don't believe I'll take any," I ventured to my tobacco spitting partner. "My father has never drunk beer or used tobacco and I don't want to either." The opportunity to be honest with myself and live in the open attracted me.

I admired many things about my dad. He set down a clear line about things right and wrong. His adherence to the old way of living and his support for the church impressed me. As a child, my conscience was largely formed by what he thought was right and wrong; my conscience was strong.

But my conscience was under attack. Friends did things I didn't want to do. I developed an insecurity that left me grappling for something to hold on to.

When I sat in church I rejoiced for the resistance my conscience had produced in the preceding days. Sermons filled with concern and deep feeling gave me motivation to do right.

But alas! I commenced compromising the guidance of the still small voice. Outside nothing changed. I did my chores, attended school, and worked. I walked the same and spoke with the same voice. My looks neither improved nor eroded. I still weighed 165. But inside; now this was another story altogether.

Why does a child's conscience erode? And when? Parents, can you see when it happens? Can it be prevented from continuing? Can we fathom the amount of TRUST it takes for a child to reveal the inner workings of the mind to an adult? What if this information could get the child into trouble; as it well could be if the conscience has been compromised? Such trust is beautiful, shining forth from the hill of understanding and communication.

A little here, a little there. Slowly the unacceptable didn't look so bad. Months after refusing tobacco, I reached for the can of Budweiser that gripped the hands of our small group of cousins. The king of beers traveled its inaugural route down my throat, after first having roughed up my taste buds. That stuff was nasty! I didn't take another swallow, but it wasn't for conscience's sake.

It tasted better the next time.

Uneasily I stilled the objections in my mind. An insecure feeling teased my spirit. I didn't know what to think. But… it wasn't too bad. The majority of my time was spent on the normal motions of human life. We brothers talked and argued. Another book was usually painting a fresh picture on my mind. I played with cousins and chatted with friends at church. Life was normal. Most of the time.

The cycle continued. Confusion brought more disobedience; more disobedience fostered confusion. Inside, a small pressure formed and grew. Rebellion followed. Outside pressure closed in as resentment grew.

As you recall, I handled all my questions and fears on my own. Confusion played a heavy hand in my brain. I taught myself to hide how I think and what I do. I didn't understand the real me, much less did I possess the knowledge how to simply BE myself. I posed, faked, put up a front. I was angry. But why should I be angry? Many reasons, be they good or bad. You fill in the blanks. What are contributing factors in the negative traits you wrestle with? How did you react to the pressing weight of youth? Me, I became isolated and angry.

A poser leads a double life. He hides himself; he hides what he does. But since he's not being honest with himself, he refuses to recognize his problems. He can't address them.

My anger ran rampant. Every once in a while when someone crossed my path, I lost it. Pressure mounted in my chest, heated words followed, the breaking point neared. The question formed, "Am I going to calm down or will I give in?" Mounting emotions surged, that *point* is reached; and then, released. Giving oneself over to screaming words of rage, yes FURY, is an experience almost euphoric at the time. Right at that point, that place where you must decide to back off or give in to this THING, the *other side* reaches out to you with welcoming arms. And then you do it. But it is so destructive. Afterward you feel drained and horrible, along with everyone within shouting distance. Do you apologize? Not often, right; only when it was especially heated. How well I remember the feeling: giving in to the ungodly passion of uncontrolled anger. The tool of the Devil! Wedges are hammered in between hearts with the iron sledge of bitter words. An invisible wall springs up. The situation deteriorates even further. Oh anger, may you be harnessed by the power of God's grace.

Chapter Four

The summer of ninety seven saw much controversy in my scramble up the ladder of life. I was sixteen years old. Unbeknownst to me, my outward rebellion was merely a cover for the things I deeply longed for: love, peace, and understanding. Tons of pressure from suppressed anger pushed the edges of my mind and fed the resentment for the authority administered by my father and the church. Way down deep my intentions were good. I wonder if anyone perceived this?! Did anyone realize I was confused and misguided? Look around you. You know someone that shares some of the traits I had at this time. Can you see past the actions; the defiance of social norms? It's easy to just write the person off because of his actions, isn't it? Or maybe, you feel what I myself did. Possibly you don't care about the opinions of others. In fact, you ENJOY the thrill of defiance. There is a certain feeling of victory in rebellion, would you not say? But look inside; a small part of you really does want to live out in the open; to actually do what the greater majority views as right.

But I was just that black sheep Wagler kid. In my secluded community, word got around. Folks knew about you. Don't think it was otherwise. So now I had to live up to the image of the community bad boy. How convenient! Now people *expected* rebellion from me. So I searched for identity in music and television. The undercover operation grew in sophistication.

Things at home changed slowly as the children grew. I mean, there was just plain a lot going on. Twenty three year old John worked up the courage to move all the way to Montana. Since David was next in line, he got to inhabit the bedroom John vacated. And he deserved it, though we didn't see it at the time. David was an organized, motivated person that got things done on the farm like neither Father nor John had been able to. He broke out of bed before five in the morning to get the eight draft horses harnessed and out into the field to disc and plow. Much as I hated it, the job fell to me part of the time as well. And Rachel happily worked around the house and yard, happy in part no doubt because of her boyfriend Lester. They spent time together Sunday evenings after the weekly youth hymn singings were over. Strict dating standards dictated that couples spend only a limited time alone with each other. Reuben and I mostly tried to stay out of work as much as possible, but we frequently had to cover for father at his sheet metal company. With business savvy he sold roofing and siding to whoever was looking for quality *and* a low price.

As summer eased into the brilliant colors of autumn, my rebellion and the opposing authority slowly built to a climax. I cared progressively less about others' opinions of me. "I'll do what I want, forget them." At times, I felt moments of genuine desire to repent and live godly. Afterward, savage regret often smothered these feelings after one of my friends or I was dealt with harshly by community people.

"Did you hear what the bishop in the other church did?" asked my friend one Sunday.

"No, what?"

"He said because George and Rosellen were seen talking at the singing they may not date for one month. Plus he grounded Jeremy and Mel for coming in late to sing."

"That's outrageous," I seethed, "how can they expect us to shape up when they're so unreasonable with us?" Hot anger danced across the face of my heart as I analyzed this injustice. I couldn't understand why we were handled like small children.

Due to my open disregard of church rules, I was often forced to stay at home while other youth gathered for singings, ballgames, etc, etc. These idle evenings provided opportunity for all sorts of mischief. At times I felt bad that I was hurting my family, but my selfish reasoning soon won over. An underlying regret always simmered deep within me, however. I was kept in check by my strong desire to spare my family more pain; that social, shameful pain that comes with close association to a disgraced member of the community. But things were primed to take a violent turn for the worst.

In early winter Reuben and I journeyed to Ottumwa to pick up his new truck, a Ford Ranger. It is important to understand that this was unheard of in our neck of the woods: two Amish boys purchasing a pickup. This was indeed a highly classified operation. In exhilaration we buzzed back home over the Iowa hills. Clearly we had just cemented our reputation among our peers as leaders of the underground revolution. No one else dared to attempt something of this magnitude. A TRUCK!!

Owning a truck intensified the underground operation as well as our opposition to authority. The pain and confusion in my heart continued to grow. I felt insignificant and unloved. Acceptance seemed to be rated by performance, and my performance was far from acceptable. I felt like nobody. No real purpose occupied my mind. No one paid special attention to me. No one could get close to my heart. A myriad of secret fears and insecurities left me feeling stupid and ashamed, thus I was compelled to rebel more in order to establish my identity. "I was Mervin Wagler, I wasn't afraid to take risks. So what if I got grounded; I had dealt with that before."

The sun was setting in defeat one cold winter evening in late November. With it, my precisely constructed world of underground operations plunged into a similar black hole. "I discovered you guys own a truck," my father told me. "Why, why? You know we can't have that. It simply can not be."

The Odyssey of a Heart

The sensibility of his authority leaped at me. My spirit rose in desperate defense as a shield against this impossible revelation. Oh the inward feeling at such a moment! A chest is not made to contain a weight such as mine had to. Emanating from my heart, an actual physical chill pervaded my upper body, choking me with a horrible dread.

How should a human heart FEEL? Ideally one would have nothing to hide. When hiding nothing, there is no fear of being revealed. That is TRUST. But what about the heart that is unable or unwilling to trust, sliding into the murky depths of deception instead? Then there is always a fear of being exposed. The heart shuts off. The web grows tighter. Every hidden action calls for another to cover up the former. It is a harsh downward spiral.

And Oh! The shock of exposure. Having backed into a corner, the heart views any action against its created reality as a direct assault on the whole person. Exposure or conspiracy to expose is the very worst of nightmares. When the brutal hand of confrontation and admonition reach out and rip the iron shield away from its secret, the heart endures timeless moments in the arctic regions of the human mosaic.

In a timeless fog of pain and frustration I stood before my dad. There simply was nothing to say. What is there to say when your actions are exactly opposite of what your father wishes them to be and then the fact is laid bare in front of you, by him? I walked away.

My mind numbly fumbled for a solution as my boots crunched the frozen dirt on the way to the barn.

The Odyssey of a Heart

"This is it, I have nothing," I calculated. "I have nothing left here; the pressure is too great. FORGET IT! I never thought I'd run away from home, but I can. I CAN! I will!" Before I had trudged the fifty yards to the barn, my mind was set.

****

On a cold Saturday night in early December, Reuben and I eased out of the house, jumped into his Ranger, and joined some friends for a few drinks. It was with an uneasy feeling that we partied that night. For starters, we had to sneak out of the house in order to make the rest of the night possible. Sneaking away into the night was nothing new for us, mind you; but you just don't get used to it. You sit in your room, waiting for things to quiet down in the house. Or you just leave before everyone's in bed. You open the window, listen, ease out onto the roof, listen, and slide down the tree if your dad hasn't cut it down in an attempt to curb your getaways; if the tree isn't there you just lower yourself down over the eave with all your weight on your hands on the edge of the roof, and you listen. You hang down as far as possible and you let go and silently fall toward the ground ten feet below, steeling your muscles for the impact. You hit the ground running and take off. The time for listening is over. Now you are outside and free to roam. Go do what you want. Go, live it up. But you can only enjoy yourself so much. You are outside the house, and that's where the problem arises. You have to get back inside! Got to get back

The Odyssey of a Heart

inside, in secret. Your parents are inside and you are deceiving them. They think you're in bed and you are not. Go, live it up, but your heart feels a dread inside of you. Party all night, but you gotta get back inside the house. It is a wretched feeling after all, this sneaking out at night. There is no peace. Sure it feels good for a bit, but tomorrow you have to fake and hide and not know if someone saw you and you'll get busted. You just don't know.

But we sneaked out of the house and went out and tore it up. We had an uneasy feeling inside, we did. But we had a pretty good time. Sure hated to think about trying to get back in the house though. Then in the early morning hours, Reuben and a buddy cruised an icy back road. Due to the impaired state of the driver, the truck slid from the road, throwing dirt and crashing onto its roof. Upon receiving a call on the then-emerging wonder of cell phones, the rest of us sped to the rescue in the almost incredibly bright glow of the full moon. At the bottom of a deep ditch beside a forsaken stretch of gravel the eerie sight of four tires reaching skyward mattered not, because my brother was unharmed. Relieved and wholly subdued we crept through the front door of home at four am, seeking the refuge of our beds.

Unfortunately this was the night my father had discovered we were gone. No doubt having just spent a sleepless night pacing the floor, he met us as we entered the silent house.

And Oh! That wretched dread, the lifeless cold feeling of exposure. Can't you feel it still? My heart was a stick of dynamite on a burning fuse.

The Odyssey of a Heart

Father wanted to talk, now. I wanted to disappear. Oh the power, the strain, of such a moment! Years of hiding, deceit, rebellion, and pain pressed upon me. The air hung around me in a dead weight.

My feet moved forward, headed for the sanctuary of my room. My mind strained under the weight of the moment... I was in disobedience; plus my brother had just survived an auto accident, causing me to ponder my actions. Now all the pain and guilt of my double life taunted me as my father busted me sneaking into the house just hours before the rising of the sun. I felt like a common criminal, lacking any good. My heart hammered a cold, vacant rhythm within my chest. I moved mechanically up the stairs to my room, which upon reaching I secured the entrance thereto and fell into the unnoticed softness of my bed. There I lay, cursing myself, life, my dad, and myself again. I teetered on the edge. The *other side* reached out, welcoming, promising relief. The breaking point loomed. The pressure in my chest threatened to choke me. I couldn't live like this any more.

My mind fought valiantly, searching for answers. It found none. Downstairs my father felt equal oppression under the weight of many unanswerable questions. Pain stalked the halls.

Resignation washed over me in a flood. "I'M OUT, gone, gone, gone. I can't deal with anything anymore. I'm out." I was leaving home as soon as possible. Nothing mattered except a release from the unbearable pressure that tightened around me.

Monday, December fifteen, nineteen ninety seven; I left home under the cover of darkness. My parents were gone for the evening. Stilling the voice of my conscience and ignoring the doubts in my mind and the obviously painful burden I was leaving at home, I walked out the door. A friend chauffeured me to his house where I would be staying. An incredible sense of freedom and power enveloped me as the Chevy S-10 sped down the highway. A new beginning lay before me. I was free from the horrible torment of a double life. I was free....

Chapter Five

The trust of a young child is a beautiful thing. Its heart is open, willing to believe no one will do it wrong. When disobedience arises it is resolved swiftly. The trust in parents is complete.

But alas, the child does not realize that his is a broken, sinful world. His parents are people with many faults; faults that often raise their ugly heads. Sooner or later he will realize those around him are not perfect.

Along about the age of ten or eleven, the child realizes father is not perfect. He is merely human. But since dad makes mistakes, he will hurt his child in some way, ever so unintentionally. The child may not realize it, but he gets hurt. His perfect trust is shaken as his heart absorbs the pain. The heart withdraws just a tad.

Since the child has no direct vision of God, he must base his perception on superiors. His guardians are always human, thus short of God. Consequently, the child begins to draw a flawed picture of God.

The Odyssey of a Heart

Every time the child experiences pain from another human above him, his heart withdraws a bit and his image of God is distorted.

Heading into the teen years, the child invariably feels insecurities and some rebellion. Parents respond; some in a good way, some in a bad way. No parent responds in a perfect way. This means the youth's heart will be hurt again. How it goes from there on out depends mostly on the parents at first. Later it is based more on the decisions the individual makes. In some cases things seem to work out with minimal problems. Other cases explode into intense pain and hatred, parents and youth worlds apart. And there is a case for every inch in between.

Once events render it so a person hardens his heart and takes his own way, the course is then determined by the person's own choices. Past is past, responsibility is now on the person himself. There is pain and it is not fair. No one gets a fair chance, but everyone deals with what they have.

Leaving the confines of the family hurdles the heart into another world; it must look out for itself. Having by now endured a fair share of pain and rejection, the heart expects more. So in order to make it in society, it must be strong. "Put up a front. Look good to your friends. Scorn heart issues. Make sure no one knows you have a soft side."

Having left the teachings of childhood behind, the youth now deals with the guilt that is piled on top of his pain. The heart backs into a corner, trying to hide so its owner won't have to deal with the issues

The Odyssey of a Heart

---

that simmer there. It's on a search, not knowing the prey it hunts. There is pain; there is a void to fill.

The turbulent waters of youth dashed on the rocks underneath the bridge of my life over the next few years. Liberation from order and authority gave me a new confidence in my abilities to tackle the obstacles around me. But my problems proved to be much too complex for me to understand. Under my locked up feelings, emotional highs and lows rolled like the waves of the sea, building pressure that I was not consciously aware of. Guilt and doubt held a strong if subtle post in my existence.

Can we understand the feeling of a bird released from a cage? All its life it has gazed through the confining spaces between the wire mesh. Time and again it has sought a way out, all to no avail. Its very existence is subject to the care of others. The spirit slowly grows dull.

But the day of freedom has arrived! The door is left unlatched, and a way of escape is ready and waiting. Oh what glorious freedoms lay outside. What should be done?

Thinking ever so hard on this fateful moment, the bird pauses to ponder the situation. "Should I take the chance? What lies beyond the safety of my cage? I could go. I want to go. But I have not a clue how life is in the great world of the fearful unknown."

With a flap of the wings it is gone.

The bird is free, but is it safe? Can it fend for itself? Other birds fly free, but is it not true that the caged one lacks the skills needed to handle the outside world?

Upon leaving home I felt like nothing if not a bird just free from a cage. Nobody told me what to do. I was intoxicated by my good fortune. If I wanted to do something, I did it. If I wanted to say something, I said it.

So I met some friends who enjoyed vandalism and theft. It didn't look like such a bad thing when I actually did it. It was a letting go, a rush. We stole tools and lawn mowers; broke windows and scratched cars. The pleasure of it all pushed us on. Defying the law offered a thrill not found in regular activities.

Directly after I left home, Reuben left as well. He and John took Reuben's beat up Ranger and headed down to Sarasota, Florida for the winter. Three of us left in quick succession; bang, bang, bang. No doubt this gouged the family deeply in several ways: not only were three of the older ones gone, we had rejected the Amish way and headed out into general society. A youth leaving the 'fold' caused heartache for the family and the entire neighborhood.

But David stayed on. He worked hard, played hard, and hunted hard.

And the younger ones filled their slots in the family and took what came.

****

At eighteen years old, I had left home twice and returned both times. I felt good about my independence- sort of. The foundation I was building on was neither solid nor secure; but I tried to keep 'er straight. And the times kept changing. Rachel got married on October 9, 1998. I had a great time talking and shouting and laughing and generally hanging out with most of my cousins. Lester and Rachel moved in next door and faced the future with a brave hope. And David still ran the show at home with the assistance of thirteen year old Glen. Mary accompanied David to the youth functions; the working bees, volley ball games, and birthday parties. And down across the state line John and Reuben installed sheet metal on old roofs.

So I moved restlessly about. I knew I needed to shape up and find the approval of man and the acceptance of God. But having experienced no inward change, living in order and subjection to authority was too great a task to endure. This did not change the fact that I honestly did want to do what was right. Upon my second return home I felt an especially pressing urge to stick it out and shape up. I wanted peace.

The ancient writings of King David in the Psalms caught my attention. Daily readings followed. Some passages almost made sense. Doing something others approved of gave me a sense of comfort.

I had many questions. Who am I? Am I normal? Do others think thoughts as I do? Does anyone care about me? Am I living right? What would my friends say if I voiced these questions? Does God hear me?

Have you ever harbored these questions within your mind? Was there a time when you needed someone to talk to; to reveal the hidden things of your heart? Ah, indeed. There was.

The Odyssey of a Heart

But what about your teenage years? Was anyone there for you? Were you a teen who bore the mark of a rebel? Are you one now? Why can't anyone see past your actions and understand that you have questions? Why do many think that you don't care at all?

I was a teen of public reproach. Fathers didn't want their sons to be my friends. Now, I wasn't bad all the time, nor was I unhappy and depressed constantly. But my actions rose high and arrested the attention of others, just as the pain within seared itself into my soul. I did as I did. I was confused.

Yes, I lived sinfully. No, elders, you can't just let youth do whatever they want. But try to *understand*. My heart lived in the midst of the fury of confusion and doubt and worthlessness. Did you know that? Were you aware of the evil forces that assailed my soul? I NEEDED you. Could you not see that? Can't you remember the outward rebellion that manifested itself so clearly? What greater sign could there be? *I needed help.*

Around you are many people, many youth that need your help. Like me, some feel anger and shame and insecurity just because it's there. There are young people around you that fight the urge to take their own life. They don't want to feel this way, but have no idea why it's there or what to do about it. They feel worthless. There are youth who are mocked, who feel like nothing. Look around you. *Understand*. There is a void.

I hurt, but I didn't cry. I didn't get angry; I didn't feel. I numbed my heart and staggered under the load of substitutes I used in an attempt to fill the chafing hollow within my heart.

I often wanted to simply have peace. I wanted to be righteous. I don't know why I didn't just yield. But what was I to yield to? No one explained to me what was transpiring inside. No one *talked* to me.

I had good intentions. Oh, you didn't notice that? My intentions were good, but didn't show in my actions, right? THAT'S BECAUSE MY HEART WAS UNCHANGED. What merit lies in following rules if the heart is corrupt?

Many people knew or told me what I shouldn't do. Usually I resented this. I wouldn't have admitted it to myself then, but I wanted someone, possibly an older person, to be there for me; to accept me as I was, without trying to change me. I wanted someone to listen to what I had to say, to try and understand my heart. I wanted someone to simply lay down their attitudes and ideas about me, and accept me without any conditions. Not my actions, just me.

Chapter Six

Then I fell in love and my world spun round,
I couldn't believe what I had found!
And my fluttering heart, it sang a tune,
My hopes flying high as the great full moon.

She was lovely to behold, and talkative. Her eyes sparkled and her voice rippled musically as she chattered with her friends. Her well placed comments showed intelligence. There were others in the room, but I had eyes for her only.

My heart thumped loudly for she turned her gaze upon me and subsequently spoke, "Haven't we met before?" she wanted to know.

"Yes we have indeed," thought I. "How could I forget?"

Ah, the powers of attraction. This pretty young lady shared some of my feeling, for later in the evening we confessed to each other the mutual attraction we felt. "How about I come see you sometime," I ventured to ask. The smile enchanted my mind and

The Odyssey of a Heart

gripped my heart. Of course I could visit. That would please her immensely.

Oh the love of youth. Who can know the limits of the passion of a heart glowing with affection for another? How can the magic of attraction be wrestled into mere word? The heart ponders the suddenly beautiful universe. On each new moment is attached another thought of *her*; the one, the only one.

We spent time, taking walks, chatting. We hung out with friends, but *she* was by far the prettiest one in the group. And why had I never noticed how musical a voice could sound? Hers was a rippling brook on a sunny spring morning.

The love for my lady was the card that trumped all others. So I'd travel out to central Illinois to see her, catching a ride with John or Reuben. Several weekends with her and I was hopelessly in love. All else took a back seat to this promise of fulfillment. The void in my heart was forgotten; I was focused.

As our relationship progressed the situation at home worsened. The crowd we hung out with possessed little respect for parents and other authority figures. Each time I left for the weekend to see my lady, I mingled with the party crowd, drinking beer and smoking cigarettes. Because these actions were far from my parents' wishes, it inevitably projected me toward a point of decision; I would have to play by the rules, or leave.

I craved acceptance and *she* filled that need better than any other source I knew. She was my hope, my stability.

The Odyssey of a Heart

I was itching to go, to move on. I elected to go to South Carolina for a while and work for my uncle Nate. Strangely enough, home turned peaceful even though my family saw it all coming. There was at least one thing I had learned from my first two departures: don't leave secretly, don't sneak out at night and force your parents to make the haunting discovery in the morning. Instead, we all knew for weeks I was leaving. It wasn't pleasant for anyone, maybe just a bit easier. The salve of courtship love covered my feelings with a comforting sheet.

I played my hole card. I left home in hopes of fulfillment elsewhere. I had great intentions. It would work. I would join *her* church. It would be great.

The very weekend I left—the very same weekend! - She broke up with me. Her brother and I cruised down the road, smoking cigarettes and listening to eighties rock. And he told me, casual like, that his sister wanted out of the relationship; it was over. She thought it would be better for us to part. We could still be friends of course.

Sucking in air, I stared through the windshield of my east bound camero as my heart staggered under the finality of this numbing verdict, my mind screaming "no, no, no." NO. All my cards lay open on the table. I went for broke and came up empty. She was gone.

"But she can't be gone," my heart screamed. "I love her. She can't just walk out of my life like that. What we had was RIGHT." Devastation pounded at my door then smashed it to pieces and invaded. Arduously I had searched for something to fill my

The Odyssey of a Heart

void and had found what I thought was love. Now it was all over; it was gone and done, it was final. An empty fog of reality crept into my brain. It was over without as much as a good bye.

Pain and loneliness saturated the following days and weeks as I toiled in the Carolina sun. I was alone again and the emptiness within was only more acute, chafing me with the razor's edge of turmoil. I was confused, still believing that being Amish and in good standing with the church was my ticket to God, but feeling cut off since I was neither Amish nor going to church. I rarely opened my Bible, though I often felt the need to. Instead I dealt with those deeper things the best I knew how: block it out, soak it up, deny it, harden your heart.

Each human heart is created with a void. This void comes into play after the person leaves childhood. A longing for something lays hold of the heart. The person usually doesn't know how to fill this void. Consequently, he attempts to fill it with whatever is close at hand: sports, friends, work, music, alcohol, drugs; it could be anything. These things never fill the void. The void was created to be filled by God.

The young person never has a fair chance. In his heart lives a void that can only be filled by God. Meanwhile his perception of God is created and continues to be shaped by his superiors. These people fall far shy of God, thereby the youth's picture of God is not always good. If the heart has taken a pattern of pain and isolation, its picture of God only becomes worse.

Every single person alive tries to fill his void with something. The heart that yields to the desire's every whim, rejecting order and authority, will feel more pain as time goes on. Often it is unaware of the wound that festers within. Occasionally the person will experience a feeling of isolation and condemnation. His heart hurts, so he hardens more. The void is unfilled.

A teenager will inevitably fall in love sometime. Suddenly someone cares exclusively about her. The heart revels in the glory of being loved. This feels like the real deal. The heart feels fulfilled.

But as often happens when a relationship ensues, it ends. The heart has to stomach another blow of pain. "This felt like the real thing, now it's gone." The heart withdraws some more. Pain grows. The void becomes bigger. It must be filled with something.

****

The mind of an Amish youth is prone to contain much confusion, as is the mind of any youth. Growing up in a conservative religious subculture raises major questions that need to be addressed. When a teenager in rebellion has questions not adequately answered, he stands on shaky ground indeed.

Early in life the Amish child is taught to obey. She has the incalculable advantage of being in a society of high moral standards. The child is taught that God is real and cares about His people. The child is also taught the importance of being Amish. How heavily this view is pushed depends on the commu-

The Odyssey of a Heart

nity, but Amish people invariably raise their children to remain Amish. This is well and good.

However, a devastating misconception regularly arises in the minds of the youngsters. They perceive that being Amish is of paramount importance. This can lead them to mistakenly think that being Amish makes one God's child, free from sin. They believe you become right with God by simply *being* Amish.

With this belief firmly entrenched in his mind, the youngster strives to deal with his problems. "I'm Amish, so I must be doing the right thing." But if his heart contains rebellion, he has no way of dealing with it properly.

Rebellion and pain are heart issues. Just doing the proper outward things helps little in matters of the heart. The one who focuses just on *doing* the right things finds himself bankrupt on heart issues. A relationship, a fellowship with God and others is needed; for without outside help, the heart won't change.

Rebellion leads to disobedience, which leads to guilt. The confused youth is unable to free himself from guilt. To be good without having a changed heart holds no peace. The web draws tighter; he drifts farther and farther from his original good intentions. On the outside he appears fine; on the inside he really doesn't care much anymore. "Oh well, I'm Amish so I should be fine."

In extreme cases, the youngster actually leaves his home and projects himself into general society. The pressure of living a double standard becomes too great; he is willing to risk damnation and leave the Amish. His anger and bitterness toward those in authority cause his heart to grow cold. The philosophy of "being Amish makes you right with God" has not held out, and he unknowingly holds this against the people who taught it to him. Paradoxically, he still believes his misinterpretation. He feels rejected and unloved as the pain in his heart feeds his rebellion.

Usually the prodigal plans to return home after a while. He understandably doesn't want to hurt his family more than he already has, and he wants to be right with God. Meanwhile; however, since he is not right with God anyway, he often goes to the extreme, doing anything he wants. Any activity becomes fair game, regardless of its acceptability by the law. "I'll rejoin the Amish later, and I'll be alright."

Many youth will eventually rejoin the Amish culture. Some remain there and later discover that accepting Christ's gift of His own shed blood for forgiveness of sins is the true way of becoming righteous, and being Amish is merely a complement; a way of living a godly life. Others remain Amish and live their lives through, believing themselves to be "righteous" because they are Amish. However, their hearts never know true peace, and their lives reflect the same. They live in a painful uncertainty of their standing on the Last Day. They want to live in paradise, but deep in their heart something is amiss.

Still others leave the culture again, and might even return a time or two. In most of these latter cases, the youth will inevitably reach a point of no return. He will discover the folly of 'just being Amish to be righteous.' His very foundation will be rocked as his one 'passage to God' lies shattered at his feet. His uncertain future stares him in the face. He is 'without God in this world' and feeling betrayed by the people who raised him. In his moral reservoir remain some good intentions, but since he no longer feels responsible to God, just empty, anything goes. The foundation for devastating bondage is laid; the clutches of sin dig in for the long haul.

On one hand the youth has unveiled a truth: simply being Amish doesn't make your heart right. On the other hand, this discovery removes much of the responsibility to do right, much of which came from the responsibility to be Amish. No clear direction remains.

I found myself mired in this third category.

Chapter Seven

If a heart is in severe pain, it often chooses drugs (or alcohol) to fill the void. This is especially devastating. Drugs provide an escape, drugs help a person feel like *somebody*. No more of this insecure fretting and wondering what other people think. While high, everything's fine.

But in between, things get worse. Guilt quietly grips the heart, for the person usually knows doing drugs is wrong. Plus, he most likely has hurt people in the past, people close to him. The effect of drugs has a way of bringing such things to the surface.

People on drugs slowly detach from the world around them. Their actions drive friends away. Feelings get hurt. To deal with this new complication, they get stoned more often. Life is unraveling; the void is not filled. Underneath simmers the pain. Underneath is the heart, crying for love; crying for someone to accept it the way it is, for someone to give a real picture of God; a real picture of something to fill the void. Alas, usually no one can see past the negative actions of the person. On he stumbles, his void is not filled…

Down in South Carolina I helped Nate build houses for rich people. We often worked at a lake front site. It was beautiful country; lakes and hills, pine trees and red dirt, and mountains on the sky line. There weren't a lot of kids to hang out with in my idle time. The ones I did hang with liked getting high, and that suited me just fine. Before the girl had entered my heart and then exited my life, I introduced myself to marijuana. This I smoked on a Saturday night as I listened to a headset radio, lying alone in my room. An overpowering rush gripped my entire body. In awe I lay without moving. I was high, and I loved it more than I had ever loved anything. I didn't smoke much over the next few months, but now I was lonely and without direction, so I hit it heavily. Getting high and mellowing out became an evening ritual. Being high assisted my escape from all things painful. My mind would cease its anguished ruminating on how I had abandoned my family. My X girlfriend couldn't touch my heart. The void in my soul was forgotten; I could live in the immediacy of being at the top of the world. All power was in my hands. I had it together. I was SOMEBODY. Many were the nights I drifted off to sleep, my body cruising through space.

Winter eased into spring, and I wanted to be closer to family back in the Midwest. David had put in his twenty one years at home and had moved to Arthur, Illinois during the winter, and Reuben joined him there. David put his motivation and organization skills to work on his own Conklin roofing business;

The Odyssey of a Heart

Reuben tried to pull his part of the business while aspiring to put himself through college. And the rest of the children at home continued to grow; life kept on humming.

John wanted help on his metal installation crew since Reuben had moved on. He called me a time or two, but I didn't need much persuading to head back up to Missouri and take up residence in John's house. John was a business man, always able to rake in the money and purchase new trucks and other pricey essentials/ wants. He owned a house and eighty acres just a bit beneath the state line. This was about forty five minutes from our parent's farm. I paid the family an occasional visit.

Oh the feel of home. Doesn't it cut through so much and serve you good memories? The lights hanging in the kitchen as the girls scramble to prepare supper: mashed potatoes, meatloaf, dressing, pie; food for a king. Mother sits on the side with a smile, her love cutting through all barriers with a true mother's affection. The pictures on the walls, the trim around the windows, the chairs round the table. HOME.

Being around my flesh and blood was great. We talked, laughed, and had a good time. But I could never shake the gnawing pain of being the black sheep. Feelings of deep pain and loss often permeated my heart as I traveled back to my abode. I always sought to become mind numbingly stoned after each visit. Pot stilled the raging torment in my mind and the rumbling torture in my heart. I needed a painkiller and used that which worked best.

As summer wore on my life continued to change. Life felt meaningful if I was getting stoned a lot; in fact, I rated the value of life by the number of times my mind and body got stoned into timelessness. The confusion, the pain, and the suppressed anger were still woven into my being; I just numbed their effect. God was still calling me, He still loved me; I just felt his urgings less. Many people felt concern for me, many people prayed; but I paid no mind. The wound in my soul was too painful, I felt too worthless, I was too confused.

Driving along highway 2 one rainy afternoon in late summer, I meditated the deep facts of life. The four rugged tires slapped out a tune on pavement worn smooth by the passage of innumerable vehicles. The twisting up-and-down highway of life hung before my eyes as well. Questions probed my consciousness.

I knew I wasn't righteous. I paid no mind to the things of heart and soul. I subconsciously believed if I would simply go home and conform to the community standards, I would be justified before God. Being Amish would do the job.

Suddenly my heart screamed epiphany. That couldn't be true! How could putting on other clothes and quitting my drug and alcohol habits justify me before God? How could church membership save me from sin? It all looked absurd. I myself could do these things. How could something I do make me righteous before God?

This revelation liberated me even while it confused me further. I still felt a responsibility to

God. That I needed to do something different was obvious. But I clearly saw that no church could possibly offer salvation. But salvation had to come from somewhere, right? I knew I was close to something real, but I knew not what it was.

So I kept getting high. Under the influence of marijuana, I didn't need to think.

****

The rain splashed persistently on the windshield on the way to work one Monday morning a few months later. Secretly I delighted in the fact that we probably could not metal the house roof on this day as planned. In our line of work we mostly dealt with sheet metal, and rain gave us mini vacations. After deliberations and driving around, the crew just happened to be close to an ATV dealership. We stopped for a tour.

All those beautiful rides! There was fun to be had and thrills to be felt on the shiny beasts of steel standing before us. Suddenly my coworker Ryan and I were ripe for spending some money.

And wouldn't you know it: on the spot financing. This was actually possible. The outrageous finance charges never registered on my young mind. We drove off the lot, each of us with a brand new four wheeler.

Speeding down a country road on my shiny new machine, wind whipping through my hair and the sweet rasp of the exhaust in my ears, I became truly alive. Thrills I wanted, and thrills I got. High speeds

The Odyssey of a Heart

in open air intoxicated my mind and stung my eyes into the bleary vision of muddled beauty. I was in control.

We lived on those 4-wheelers over the next few months. A ritual smoking of pot preceded each ride, after which we rode the local hills and gullies with the wild abandon of minds mellowed and senses hungry for adventure. We attacked hills, jumped ditches, crashed our rides, and endured pain on each outing. Life felt just fine.

I met the love of my teenage life, meth, on a Friday night in October. Long had I wanted to make her acquaintance, and now someone had been able to score about a gram of powdery brown crank. I was unaware that it was made of chemicals, that it feeds on the central nervous system, and that it can cause permanent brain damage. I did not know it destroys relationships, causes extreme mental torture, and has contributed to crime and suicide. I only knew I loved getting stoned, and this was my ticket to the next level.

So I got to spend some time with this sleeping monster of meth. She looked so small and innocent. She hinted nothing of the powers that lay within her chemical bowels. I snorted her off the counter top and smoked her on a foil. She made me feel like a man, with the power to stay awake all night. I fell in love, with all the passion of one who has been searching for the right one and has just laid eyes on a beauty like none other. She whispered sweet lies into my ears.

The Odyssey of a Heart

The following Sunday several of us went off-roading again. With the memory of my lady meth still fresh in my senses, I snorted the last of the chemicals. She began her work quietly, and by the time I hit the trails the iron rush of her powerful grip sped through my veins. That afternoon of riding was the best I ever had, hands down. I rode without an ounce of fear; up hills, down gullies, and in creeks. I cut donuts and popped wheelies. And I jumped.

A dry pond lay at the top of a lonely hill. On one side the bank dropped sharply about five feet to the bottom. This I converted into a launching pad, coming from the other end with my 300 cc Kawasaki rapped out in third gear. I was invincible. I was the hero of every movie ever made. I was da man. Nothing had ever matched the sensation of the shocks recoiling as the tires bit black dirt, down from the lofty heights of a second before. I rushed the bank time and again.

Numerous such jumps exhausted my mind and body. Deciding to quit, I roared up to the truck.

"Well, why not one more jump?" my lady meth whispered. "I'll give you another thrill if you wish."

I had mentally wound down and didn't have enough thrust as I sailed into the air for the last time. Ten feet up I detected a drastic problem as the nose of my ride tilted downward at a crazy angle. I fought for balance, but the nose dived down into violent contact with the earth rushing up to meet us. My body catapulted forward as the back wheels overtook the front ones.

Then... slowly my mind struggles to focus. Gray... I am trying to move, but the 4-wheeler is on

The Odyssey of a Heart

my arm. Voices float around me. Faces swim above me. I try to understand why I am in this crazy land of gray.

The fog clears a bit as the ATV is lifted from my arm. I sit up slowly, painstakingly, giving plenty of grace to my right arm, by now in considerable pain. I look around in a daze, there are people around me but they are detached somehow, not part of the big picture. I stare at my right arm; stare at the lump on the mid forearm. My arm has an angle where there was none. Calmly I suggest we seek the services of the nearest hospital. With high speeds we are there in a few minutes.

My head cleared a bit as I sat in ER answering questions. After an hour at the local band-aid station, an ambulance rushed me to University Hospitals in Iowa City. Late that night a team of doctors set my arm, mercifully popping my elbow back into its socket as well. One bone in my forearm was broken cleanly, requiring the additional support of a six inch metal plate and half a dozen screws.

By the next morning I lay in a regular hospital bed, watching ESPN. I had not a care in the world as the prescribed morphine did her quiet work in the halls of my bloodstream. I was high once more. Further, I knew I would be prescribed powerful legal drugs to fight the pain from my operation. "This isn't so bad," I thought. "Now I can be high all the time."

Thus began a rapid downward spiral that would threaten to take everything from me, even my very life.

Chapter eight

The now barren country side of central Iowa slipped past my window as my two friends and I cruised home from the hospital. A weak sun filtered through the bare trees on the Monday morning scene. I reflected on the events of the past weekend. There I was with a busted arm, no money, and newly unemployed. Furthermore, I was a bit uneasy, for the ambulance crew from the night before was aware that I had been on meth at the time of the accident. The local police had been keeping their eyes on me for some time, their suspicions aroused by the company I kept. Would the hospital staff tip off the cops?

We concluded that no ethical hospital would betray their patients. With this comfort the conversation turned to more pressing matters: would I be able to do meth now, considering my accident? Would the drugs slow the healing process?

A stop at the pharmacy produced the stout painkillers I would need over the next few weeks. I popped a couple and waited for the warm buzz in my stomach. It came quickly. "This is great," I thought gleefully, "legal drugs." The world became an agreeable place as we neared home.

Pulling in sight of my house, a horrifying scene shocked our senses dumb. About eight patrol cars were parked all over the yard; cops swarmed the place. I literally could not believe my eyes.

Cursing and swearing erupted within the truck as we sped past. I was usually a laid back guy, but I lost it. And John the easily excited one went into a frenzy. He knew I had his house loaded with illegal stuff: most heavily on my mind weighed the eight pot pipes and the meth hitter that were inside the house that Scotland County's finest had now besieged. "How beautiful," I muttered, throwing my fake ID out the door. "I've got a broken arm, no money, no job, and now I'm in trouble with the law." My mind operated slowly, clearly as we circled back and turned into the drive; into the jaws of the United States justice system.

After returning from the visit downtown, I relaxed on the couch. The effects of the oxy codeine soon drifted me off to a place of quiet comfort. My life had complicated itself immensely, but I wasn't sweating it just yet.

Waking up the next morning, reality threw me a left hook right to the brain. First order of business was to acquire the services of an attorney. With some references I hired a St. Louis lawyer that did rural practice as well. I desperately wanted reassurance from him, of which he gave me none at all. "Oh well," my mind deadpanned, "might as well get stoned."

The Odyssey of a Heart

Such advice sounded just dandy, so I followed it wholeheartedly.

Since my mind stayed stoned, I did not perceive that perhaps God was speaking to me. By the weekend after my accident I was ready for more chemicals. Stopping by my supply point, I got cranked up on a good dose of meth. Grabbing about a gram more I headed out of state for the weekend. After partying for a few days I headed back home to reality. However, I greatly valued the ease of forgetting all my troubles while on meth.

For the next few weeks I sat on the couch, watching TV and staying stone high on the drugs available to me. Night blended into day as I started losing all sense of time. I didn't have to do a thing, be anywhere, just nothing at all. The only thing to do was exist and get high… The die was cast, the downward spiral begun.

****

Now I cruise through the night of rushing sensations and isolation. Eventually I reach my destination in the early morning hours. It took me ages to travel the two hundred miles. Or was it only a few hours? I watch TV, drink a beer, drift off to sleep.

The next day I get stirring about noon. I don't go seek out many people; instead a few select stoner friends are my companions on a weekend of cruising back roads, toking up, doing lines, and zoning. Late at night it is the parties, music loud and drinks all around. Meth breaks down my reserves and I can talk to anyone, to the girls. I love it.

I stay wide awake most of the weekend then travel home and sleep for a few days.

Time passes in a haze. My weekend road trips begin stretching into the week. I lose all sense of time. Occasionally I think of God, feeling a gnawing uneasiness at my present state. These promptings from my conscience usually fade with my next indulgence into chemicals. I've a vague awareness that I am slipping into a strange and dangerous place. Coming down off meth highs, my very being is tortured with regrets about life, my inactivity, and how far I have drifted from my family. But usually meth is the only thing that matters.

The next months are a blend of events: I'm in my room, high as a kite and smoking a joint. I roam the floor restlessly as the effects of the chemicals already in my system grip my mind and body. The walls dance before my eyes and the wood grains on the nightstand appear in minute detail. All things feel close yet far away. I feel like I'm in control, but still lack control. On a stand lies the Bible my parents gave me for my twelfth birthday. I stare at it as memories from another time and place prick my consciousness. A feeling something like fear and respect pass through me. I feel a deep awe for this book, but don't touch it. My life is too far off track for me to even lay hands on a Bible, I muse.

I cruise a lonely stretch of I-70, my left hand resting easy on the wheel of a half ton Silverado. My body rushes through a place of no gravity as a combination of meth and pot course through its system. My chest quivers against the racing of my heart, telling me I have now escaped time. Nothing matters. My life is extremely complicated. Adversity nips at my heels. But I simply DON'T CARE. All those things are so infinitely far away right now. I'm cruising the interstate, not a living soul knows where I am. I'm alone. Very, very alone. Nothing matters; I'm exactly where I want to be. The throaty rasp of the exhaust arrests my ears as smoke drifts from the joint I'm killing. The clock shows two AM as I float in a world of no reality except the present moment.

I walk restlessly in my house, feeling a vast emptiness in my soul. I have been awake for the most part of three of four days. Now I am 'coming down', rapidly descending to lows of unfathomable depths. A vicious hollow gnaws at my chest, removing all reason and purpose in my life. My very body feels empty, hollow; as if there is simply nothing there. I feel utterly horrible, contemplating my life in general. I scurry around the room, cleaning it up, focusing; trying to fabricate some kind of structure, something to distract me from the torment that floods my being. Nothing works. Nothing, absolutely NOTHING about my life looks positive. Tears press my eye lids as I contemplate the gulf that separates me from everyone else. I ruminate my childhood and the pain I'm causing my family, my soul weeping the voiceless pain of isolation.

On a cold January night I take my first hit of acid. Three of us sit around in the kitchen, sucking on tiny squares of thin cardboard soaked in the drug. Within

The Odyssey of a Heart

the hour I am gripped by the power, floating- and I mean REALLY floating- through time and space. It is profound to sit and literally to move, to fade away. Later we hit the road in a ford T-bird. I sit in the back next to the speakers pounding out music like I have NEVER heard before, the fact that I know quite a few of the songs notwithstanding. I feel as if I'm surrounded by a wall fifty feet thick. This place is shockingly timeless. Reality permits only the present, and the present makes me very happy indeed.

The next day I awake a changed person. Everything I see stands out in greater detail than before. Life now holds a mystical power. LSD has touched my brain and I want more.

A week later I travel hours to get this drug again. I pop a few hits late at night before driving back towards home. The landscape dimly visible could be the moon for all I know. At the dawning of a new day with Jimi Hendrix jamming guitar, the hills rise up in a deep purple and my heart swells within, trying to grasp the grandeur of it all. We float onward in a fuzzy yet crystal world.

I am engulfed by the combination of drugs I use. I don't resist their power. When they speak I listen. I want to be high all the time.

A few more days, a few more weeks, a few more highs. I get hooked up with a pretty decent stash of acid one Friday night out in Illinois. Three of us make a purchase and drop by our friend's house for the night, where we can 'trip' in a safe environment. Tonight we're into big doses, buddy. It's mellow and electric and thrilling and GNARLY. We sit around, tripping wildly, talking, watching TV; sitting in our little cubicles. The colors, they are awesome, they flash and blend. It's all good.

And after a while three of us go into the back bedroom of the trailer home and break out a bit of meth. The senior druggie lays out a few rails for us on the top of a chest of drawers, and we snort that chemical right up the nose. Take it in, feel the burn, screw up your face, and pound your head into the air. Then he brings out the light bulb and loads it and gets the smoke drifting lazily. But I don't know, friend. My mind can see right through everything around me, and the smoke coming of the light bulb carries the stench of hell. It is fearsome and foreboding. Never have I felt this way. Something is wrong.

The bulb is handed to me. I hold it and stare into it. Of a sudden I see things clearly. This drug on the glass is the god I pray to, the one I serve. We are in the midst of some unholy, ancient ritual, something dark.

It feels wrong, and I'm scared. But I take a hit.

Daylight sneaks into the trailer the next morning and I am still wide awake. One of the guys got way too much acid last night and fell asleep early, curled up on a bed. Now he's comes out of the bedroom, looking like death incarnate. "I'm never doing that stuff again," he mumbles.

The day drifts by, and we cruise around, smoking some weed and drinking a few beers. I score some coke later in the evening and the ride continues into Sunday. I'm two nights without sleep by the time I head back toward Missouri Sunday evening, driving

The Odyssey of a Heart

down I-72 and working the attentive gas pedal of the ole' Dodge Caravan. I grow tired as the staying-awake power of meth fades away. I pop a hit of acid as freezing rain commences to fall. The windshield fogs and I stare into the inky blackness. Switching to a two lane road, I am confronted by oncoming headlights. The pupils of my eyes are wide open, unable to even see the road in the glare of each southbound car we meet. I just try to keep her out of the ditch and on my side. The road becomes icy.

Driving north on the icy pavement of state road 61, I observe my life from a vantage point beyond human. Meeting autos with their blinding lights, I focus in utter absorption. As I zone I see myself in this place called the United States, driving the only road within her borders. I contemplate my life as a drug user, the life possessed by the chief desire to do drugs; to do drugs and to continue so until death. And death seems to be my lot in my twenties, I believe. Shouldn't be too bad though. I'll just stay high.

But I do get close to home tonight after all. The leftover cocaine from the weekend should be shared, so I stop by Ryan's house to spread the joy with him and his girlfriend. Driving up to the house, I jump out of the faithful van and meander across the yard. Ryan greets me at the door and shows me in. After having driven for hours with LSD on my brain, the mere act of walking affects me immediately. The world around me pulses with sounds and colors, with intensity. I walk into the living room and plop down on the couch.

Now, I have just spent two days and three nights wide awake, with no sleep at all. My brain and body are still loaded with the chemical intake of the weekend, and I'm feeling just fine. What I'm saying is, I feel no pain whatsoever at this precise moment. I am in the ZONE. But my friends at the house are feeling exactly the opposite. I sense a powerful oppressive presence as I step inside. My heightened awareness tunes in to the atmosphere of the house. Something is wrong, very wrong.

Apparently my friends feel betrayed by someone they trusted and are generally down on their luck. Extreme depression has laid hold of their souls as they come down from several weeks of a constant meth high. Life holds no purpose for them. A hellish emptiness of soul has struck with brutal force, knocking their spirits senseless. They slouch on the couch, utterly discouraged, lacking even the will to live. After a line of coke and a passing of miserable timelessness they drift off to sleep muttering, "Oh, that I would never have to wake again." The girl's five year old son curls on a ball on the recliner, whimpering like a lost puppy. A live THING grips the house. A raw ugly reality of darkness and pain permeates my whole being.

I walk from the house knowing I have been in the manifest presence of the spirit of evil assaulting the human soul. My innocent reality disappears, just like that. My mind fights the overwhelming pressure of this unprecedented distress. All I want is to be happy and have a good time.

My mind trips wildly in the acid reality of my mini van on the final leg of my endless journey home through the storm of ice and snow, through the frigid winter of my soul. Brother John listens carefully as I explain my troubles to him. He is keenly aware that I am in a place he can only imagine.

"You need to leave for a while," he says. "Why not go back to Carolina and work for Uncle Nate?"

I consider this. "No, I don't want to leave. I'm tired of always moving around all the time. I want to stay in one place for a while. And I'm still in trouble with the law here."

John is not convinced. He clearly sees I am in way over my head with all the drug stuff. The environment in SC where I don't know too many people would be much better for me. "You need to go," he repeats.

Two days later I am sober again. With a clear mind I ponder the craziness of drugs that swirls around me, my trouble with the law, the dangerous people I deal with, and the wrenching depression of my friends. Further, I often feel nasty myself. John's idea makes a lot of sense. I'll go. I'll escape.

Three days later I head south. I stop by David and Reuben's house and hang out for a few days. I search out a few of my cronies and we get high and wired. With only two hours of sleep in three days I head on to SC Sunday forenoon. My meth supply is gone and I only have pot and acid. Plus, a severe cold is entrenched deep within my throat, which soon becomes much too sore to inhale smoke. I can't smoke pot and my energy deteriorates fast as I speed along. It is going to be a long ride.

I rapidly sink to being deathly ill as ragged coughing shakes my body again and again. I stop at Cracker Barrel and enjoy breakfast food as the room floats around me. I can't concentrate on the questions posed by the waitress; it seems like the people are staring at me and I swear I hear my name from somewhere. I hit the road and soon pop another hit of acid in a desperate attempt to gain some energy. Instead it only heightens the pain inside my body. My very bones grind against each other. On I-24 between Nashville and Chattanooga the van and I labor up a long grade. Up and up we go and on and on we travel, slowly and speedily, with a focus and in a fog. Then it is on down the other side, losing altitude rapidly down the steep grade past the rock walls and the runaway truck ramps. My ears are popping and I'm barreling down the Interstate. My bones ache, my muscles groan, my whole being labors; trying to keep the engine inside of me running. And down we go as I slowly drift off into oblivion. I'm in the middle lane, almost to the bottom of this long hill. We round a sweeping curve, me and the two semis I'm sandwiched between do. And my ears pop, then I'm hanging by my ears and I'm going around the curve with a Peterbilt on my right and a Kenworth on my left, and I can't feel the gas or the wheel. All I feel is the rod jammed through my head as I hang here in my van. My bones hurt and I cough a ragged cough. I need to focus or I'm going to get killed. God, help me through this!

Fear clutches me by the throat, telling me I **MUST** focus and not die. I must feel the wheel and stay in control. I listen, then ease off the gas and allow the trucks to cruise on ahead. I creep into the right lane and keep my speed down.

The road is long and flat and I am SO tired. I'm tired of coughing and I'm tired of grinding my bones against each other; I'm just tired. The white lines keep on coming at me, solid on the right and broken on the left. I am so tired. The road goes on into the darkness.

I awake and I am driving down I-24. I awake on the middle of the road and I am crowding a car onto the shoulder. My heart leaps and slams my mind to alertness. I must focus. I must keep my eyes open.

But I am so TIRED.

I am deathly ill, my body run down by months of chemical abuse. I just know this is the night I will die. I can feel it. I envision passing out and crashing into the ditch. Many motels wave at me from the side of the road, but I lack the capacity of mind to pull over and sleep. I imagine what death will be like. A terrible aching loneliness fills and chills my soul. I am all alone in the middle of nowhere; I must die alone.

Chapter nine

After a few years of ignoring the issues inside, the heart has built a wall of defense. It may not realize what is transpiring. It does not understand how to process painful situations, and therefore bottles them all up inside.

And sometimes it turns to meth. The heart is now in considerable pain. It has felt the sharp edge of rejection, the dull pain of isolation, and the raging torment of guilt. The whole mosaic of experiences sits in the heart, sits and waits.

Enter meth. Here is an incredible escape. A place of no past and no future! How convenient. The brain and heart are distracted. But meth gets things happening, the wrong way. Given time, something bad will happen. This is often a thing most unpleasant for the mind to meditate on. What to do?

Such a question! Get high, of course. But living in a chemical world, old memories and old hurts surface with renewed vigor. The unresolved pain only becomes worse. Compounded with the difficulties of late, the situation can appear very daunting indeed.

At this point the heart has lost most of the faith in itself. Since mostly negative things are occurring, more of the same is expected. Other people provide little or no help.

Time marches on. The heart often feels happy. Normal everyday life isn't too bad. Friends are close by. The highs feel good while they last. But in those ever increasing moments, those moments of acute pain; the emptiness within hangs vast. Pondering life, a bitter, helpless feeling arises. Life is spinning out of control; the heart is raw, bleeding, in pain….

I make it to my home in Seneca deep in the night after an epic twelve hours on the road. Cruising down outta Tennessee and into Georgia, my mind had pretty much given up on me. But sprawling Atlanta gave me hope; I was only a few hours from home. Roll the rubber over the wide lanes of the 85 bypass and I was heading east again. Out into the country on the ribbon of concrete, out into the country past the all night gas stations toward the hills of Carolina. Thirty minutes from the house I realized I was almost out of gas. I prayed the station on my exit would be open. It wasn't, I hit the two lane roads, trying to think of something to tell the cop that finds me sleeping in my van on the side of the road. But the old engine kept purring along, below the orange line and gone.

I make it. I roll into town and put about five dollars in the old workhorse. That gets me the last few miles home. I drive into Uncle Nate's place and kill the engine and sit and stare vacantly, then stumble out of the faithful Dodge and walk to the house. I have never been so exhausted. I am much more than just strung out; my system has been fighting the ill effects of my bad habits for far too long.

Nate shows me in and seats me on the easy chair in the living room. The TV runs on some late night show. My host crashes around the kitchen, getting me sweet tea and hot chili, and asking questions. We sit in the living room around the coffee table, and I try to hide the fact that I am high and strung out and just really out there. I drift off to sleep, but not before I hear Nate mutter, "That boy wouldn't have made it another half hour."

I fall asleep and I sleep deep, way deep. I awake in a haze and it is daylight outside. I lie there feeling no energy at all, just tiredness. I go to the restroom, get a drink, and fall back into my bed under the pool table and I'm gone. It is a deep sleep again, exhausted sleep. I wake and it's dark and I fall asleep and awake and it is daylight and I fall asleep again. And I awake and Nate has some soup prepared and orders me to consume it. But I'm not hungry and I don't want to eat. I just want to lie here and sleep. I'm tired, can't you see? Yes I know, but you've been there for two days now.

I fall asleep.

After two days and two nights I am strong enough to get out of bed and stomach some food. Nate orders me to visit the doctor and get some pills to help balance my system. It is good to be moving about, doing what normal humans do. I actually have to go outdoors and accomplish a task. Nothing like

The Odyssey of a Heart

a little structure to get you back in gear. My sense of purpose and schedule was way down: time of day meant nothing; day of the week meant even less. Now the journey back has to begin.

Nate looks out for me these first days; he has a real concern for me at a time I need it most. And he knows I am living dangerously. "Don't ever come to my house in that condition again," he admonishes me. To Nate I am forever indebted. I went to him when I could find no where else to turn.

Several days after arriving in SC I feel well enough to smoke a joint and go on a cruise into the country. The foothills lie in the splendor of the sun setting over a large lake. In the distance the mountains raise their heads over the various shades of ridges and valleys. Orange and blue and green and black, and the white of distant mist. I grip the wheel and press the gas. I feel human again. I might even BE human again, after the torture of a months long head trip on meth. This is my land. The beauty soaks through me and thrills me and calms me, it brings tears to my eyes. I am home.

****

The Carolina sun rises over the foothills. In the cup is coffee, black. The music plays to the strains of an old Dwight Yoakam traveling tune. I feel a bit of energy in me as I head to work for the first time in months.

Nate's crew is constructing a lake front house for a local doctor. Standing three stories tall with various hips and valleys up top, it is an impressive sight as I drive up and park among the old beaters out by the road. Must be the boys have already gathered.

I meet the guys before we get to work. Quite the bunch: a college kid from Clemson, an ex army sergeant, a seventeen year old kid, a fifty year old day laborer, a guy fresh out of prison, and a red head named Thomas. Thomas is my age.

It should be an interesting first day.

Hours later I wearily climb the hill to the van. I have swung a hammer, run the saw, and scrambled on the roof. My first real project is rather complex. I had to bring two hips and two valleys together in mid air and tie them all together in a peak. Sure had to use my mind on that one, and I'll have to use it some more in the morning. I'm hoping it'll look good when it's done, especially since the boss just said go do it and didn't give any instructions.

I'm back to work the next day, and the next, and the next. Exercise, exercise. Yea!

And I keep smoking on the half pound of pot I brought down with me. I know a few kids from college who smoke, so we hang out and mellow out. I need to get buzzed daily to retain the relative calm in my spirit, to keep my normalcy. I wait till after hours, though. Need to stay straight at work.

I try not to think of all the craziness back home. Did all that stuff happen? I wonder. Did I really see those kids in all that misery, in that hopelessness and emptiness? Seems I did. I know my friends are doing battle with what can only be evil, and I can do nothing about it. I prefer to light up some good

The Odyssey of a Heart

bud and just forget it all. I mean, I started getting high because I liked being carefree. I like getting high because nothing matters then, the heart feels no pain. Now don't start telling me about people all tore up and depressed and not wanting to live. That's complicated. Keep it simple.

On top of all that, I worry about the law. Months have passed since the police besieged my house, and nothing has happened further. It is now reasonable to believe the matter will not be pursued, but...

My only solid contact outside SC is my three older brothers. I can always call them. But the thought of my two younger brothers at home without my being there, that's a thought that dogs me at odd moments, day and night. More so at night. Light a joint....

****

"Want a cigarette?" I ask Thomas one day. I notice he hardly smokes besides an occasional one.

"Don't believe I do," he says.

"That's cool, don't be afraid to ask."

The lake glistens in the mid morning sun. Nice weather.

"Actually I'm trying to quit," ventures Thomas, "I don't see a lot of good coming from it."

Admirable. Nothing wrong with that. I quit once but it didn't last for long. Good if someone can break the yoke, though.

Later I invite a few of the guys over for some drinks. Thomas declines, saying he doesn't drink either.

The Odyssey of a Heart

My confidence is on the rise. One day Nate tells me I've now matured into a genuine carpenter. I hang on to that compliment for days. Someone has acknowledged some good within me. Structure is returning to my life, bit by tiny bit. I mean, I actually have to get out of bed in the morning!

It's going quite well, I'm feeling good, I've got the ole' conscience pretty much quieted down. I've got a little money in the bank, I'm hanging out with friends; camping in the mountains, cruising the lake, cruising the roads. Then I get a call from up north, telling me the old home farm will be sold and my family is moving their metal business out to the highway. The farm with its hills and ravines and draws, its woods, fields, streams, ponds and fence rows; will be sold to some stranger who will come in to inhabit the house, to use the buildings, to change whatever it is he wishes, and LIVE THERE! An outrage! I feel sad, I feel a bit guilty, and then I feel downright horrible. I've abandoned the family and they simply can't run the farm alone. Now it will be sold away, this place of so much joy, this place of so many regrets and a sense of loss. It's like my turbulent teen years are being sold away and I can't return to make the wrongs right.

My family encourages me to travel to Iowa for the March twenty fourth auction, but I decide to remain in Carolina. I am not ready to go back and face everyone and everything. I just kinda hang loose and try to keep my mind as happy as possible.

On a Saturday night in early March, 2001, I cruise to my friend's house at the local college campus. I've

The Odyssey of a Heart

been down here over a month now, and I've got a steady job that has restored some semblance of order to my life. I haven't done any of the mind burning chemicals lately but I smoke weed all the time. Life is pretty good; I feel more positive that I have in a long time. But on this night I want meth, I want it bad, I want it NOW. I will not deny myself.

Well, you can't just go buy this stuff wherever you want. You need to know somebody. I know somebody who knows somebody. I go hang out at his house, where a dozen kids are already getting right for the night. Come meet this guy, says Smoky. Want some rock, huh. Sure I can get some. How good is it? Good stuff, maybe not the best you've ever had but I guarantee it'll trip your head out all night long. How much you want? A fifty spot. Okay, I'll be back.

I guess I could have gotten a full gram but a half will sure do for now.

The dude is back after an hour. I lay that stuff out and Oh, is it ever sweet, the burning and the numbness. I share some with a guy I never saw before. It's all good. I sit around, zone, snort some more. We play cards deep into the night and talk inside that loving and fuzzy timeless capsule. I am on a WIRE.

As the sun rises over the mountains hours later, several of us are deep in the hills by a huge waterfall, drinking in the wild beauty around us. I'm in something larger than myself, this mystical place of power and beauty. There's a certain kind of electric thrill, a rush deep in my chest that comes from pushing across the line of the safe world, over to here where brave people like myself dare to defy convention, family, even God Himself. We dare to live in a chemical reality.

I find it hard to describe the state I'm in up here on the mountain this morning. It's partly awesome and partly foreboding. If you've gotten high like I have, you know. If you've never snorted a line or hit the bulb, you can't know how it is and you can't know how lucky you are for it. It's the feeling that will haunt you years down the road as you sit and watch your kids play and think back to the old days; and of a sudden the forgotten, the forbidden fruit of chemical timelessness will tease you and you'll feel that lonesome feeling inside, but you'll be OK — you pulled through the hard times.

But on this morning cruising down off the mountains my spirit is restless from a pounding heart and a racing mind. Meth is up to her old tricks again. I stay on the move most of the day before easing down come evening. Nate is not amused. He is highly suspicious of my all night activities. Darkness comes, I try to relax and get some sleep, the sleep I didn't get last night. Got work tomorrow. But my mind is still wired. I lie on the couch and watch TV but the colors all blend into one; they blend into orange, into fire. Man, why did I have to go screw everything up again?

Work is a disaster the next day. I can't focus, I have no energy, and I hate myself for being a weakling and getting high. Life no longer feels good at all. My spirit's all tore up. I think of my father's auction with a sweeping wave of regret. At quitting time I go home and rest, trying to generate some energy.

The Odyssey of a Heart

I sleep, awake, and go to work. Then I do it again. And again. I have no motivation or energy till Friday, when I can finally focus a little. That meth must have been some nasty stuff. Wiped me out for four days.

I spend the weekend in a crazy assortment of dreams filled with guns, fighting, and death. Skeletons rise from the ground to chase me. Soldiers armed with machine guns fire my way. I am all alone in a place of evil and confusion, fighting for my life. The universe once again spins backward and out of control.

As I labor away on Monday I try to wiggle my way out of the mental crisis I'm in. Perhaps I could travel to Iowa after all? I'm unfocused and merely tolerating work. I need to get away. I believe it's time to hit the road.

Early Thursday I strike out across the great US of A, heading up to the Midwest. The good ole' road sooths my soul and I relax behind the wheel. The longing to see the folks starts burning inside me as I cruise through Georgia. The miles of interstate disappear beneath the hood; the memories of other roads and other times play with my head. Cravings for meth scratch at my mind as I long for that place of timelessness. The miles stretch longer. I know meth is waiting back home, and there I set my sights. Cigarettes and music preoccupy me as I envision the good times that await me.

Hours later in the early morning of the next day I reach my destination. I cruise right on over to the man I know and we break out the powder, the drugs. The hours on the road fade away, the chemicals make

The Odyssey of a Heart

me forget my fatigue, and I rest in the warm embrace of heavy drugs once again. I love this feeling!

My friends on heavy depression have changed not at all in my two month absence. On the contrary, they have sunk to almost incredible depths of evil forces and screaming voices, suffering the effects of the devil's handiwork. Mentally tortured to the limit, they exist in the hellish reality of no hope, in terror of everything around them. I am ill prepared for what I meet.

The human body is a wonderful creation. It boasts numerous amazing functions to help out its inhabitant throughout life. In order to stay healthy, the body needs adequate rest and nutrition. A sick body can easily lower the spirits and make one susceptible to negative thoughts. The mind works in the same way, only with higher stakes.

A weary mind is conducive to a gloomy outlook. Lack of sleep makes people cranky. But however tired the mind is, it can easily be refreshed with a good night's sleep.

A person using meth gets little sleep. The mixture of chemicals hardwires the brain, rendering it unable to recognize the need for rest; meanwhile, the mind works overtime to accommodate the experience of staying stoned. After several days of no sleep, the world becomes a strange place indeed. The mind is exhausted for the lack of rest but it must press on. It can no longer function properly and does not see things the way they actually are. It only wants meth, and if it's available, the journey continues.

The Odyssey of a Heart

After a week of being awake, the mind can be severally incapacitated. Paranoia often sets in. The person feels like a victim, for he is unable to cope with the normal events of life. At this point the devil finds easy access to the reality the person now lives in. Voices will sound in his head, tormenting him day and night. More time passes and the person feels everyone is out to hurt, even kill him. Eventually he lives in a world no one else can see. To him it is real; he knows nothing else. The devil whispers in his ears, and he thinks it is God. The medical profession has labels for this, but it is the fruit of the powers of darkness. The person that spends weeks high on meth is living in the active forces of evil. Such is the situation I find.

Chapter ten

The clock shows four AM. An obscure movie runs on the TV. Outside an occasional car rattles past. Inside, two men sit on a distant plane of meth induced visuals. Time does not exist.

"They're after me," says Ryan, "they keep coming and I have to fight them all the time. I've killed two of them this morning already."

A strange foreboding grips me, just like that. What is going on? What can this guy be talking about? Ryan sits across from me, wearing a tired, yes, even hunted look.

After a while, "Who's after you?"

"Everybody, all the time. They come for me any time I let my guard down. I hear them all the time; when I don't listen they try to kill me."

I sit dumbly. Where this is all coming from I can't begin to understand. I don't know if actual people are intent on killing Ryan or if it's the mental and spiritual sub reality. Whatever it is, it carries the stench of darkness and hopelessness.

The Odyssey of a Heart

"Nobody believes me," says Ryan. "I'm all alone. Every day I must fight these evil things and no one believes me. They've all turned against me." Silence fills the room as my once simple life becomes titanically more confusing by the minute. Ryan is in the grips of some great evil; that much is obvious. No one believes him. Except me. The evidence lies not. What can I do?

"I believe you," I assure him. Someone needs to validate the torment this guy is in. He is way out there. "I know it's for real," I repeat.

The movie drones on as silence reigns once more. I have always denied the existence of spiritual powers. Now I am confronted by evil. My friend lives in a reality unimaginable to most everyone else. For some reason I get a clear view of the other side. Deal with it I can not. My mind screams for a solution as a dark force lays hold of my heart.

Bang, bang, bang goes the second hand up on the clock. Is every click a second, or is it a minute? Maybe it's a lifetime. Wait a minute, isn't time stopped completely? But the hands are moving, not so? Sure, but that doesn't say time is. Did I just say time? What kind of word is that? I've never heard of time before.

We need to hit some back roads, bad. The walls confine the troubled zoning we are in. Out to the van, bang the doors. The March morning is dreary, nondescript.

Cruising the back country, my mind struggles to find something of substance to say to Ryan. A quiet desperation hangs about him. He is hunted and he's been all alone with the knowledge for weeks. The desire to understand him nearly chokes me, but at the same time I resist it. The demons at work haunt me as well. I want away, far away.

'They're trying to steal my soul," he says. "I have almost no good thoughts left. They want to take all my good thoughts. When I have none left, they will take my soul as well. I can't do ANYTHING to stop them." His eyes are wild, looking past me.

The next few hours we cruise the hills as a world opens up to me that can't be real. But it is real. Ryan's world has crumbled. He thinks everyone is against him. He hears numerous voices in his head, terrorizing and condemning him. He thinks the physical humans around him want him dead. And the voices are trying to take his soul. The fear is absolute. He can not distinguish reality from the voices screaming in his head. As we cruise and smoke joints, the devil sits with us, his presence as real as that of our own.

The petty routines and habits of life fade into oblivion. We are in the midst of a battle of Good and evil; the stakes are our very souls. My mind works slowly, painfully, searching out a solution. Hopelessness engulfs me. This evil is far greater than any other force I've ever known. It floods me with a raging torment, condemning me for my life of unrighteousness. But even as the evil strengthens, God becomes real as well, faintly visible through the fog. It is a glimmer of hope, almost to dim to see. But I can't attain unto it.

"We could go to church," I volunteer as we drive state road 136. "Maybe we could find help there." In my mind's eye I see this might be something to make the evil go away. We just simply can't fight it alone.

Ryan stares out at a few naked trees standing on a lonely hill. His eyes almost dare to hope. "Yes, I've thought of that, I'd like to go."

Keep 'er between the lines. Take a sip of water, smoke the joint. Think. Stare at the road, the sky, the hills. Stare into your soul. Smoke the joint. Talk. Think, and try to control the racing it brings to your mind. Cruise the road, cruise those old Missouri roads, and try to think good thoughts. Smoke the joint, smoke the Marlboro light, and by God, try to think good thoughts... The day passes, one frame after the other. Brother John is happy to see me back but alarmed at the company I'm in. He knows things have gotten crazy beyond belief, but he doesn't know the half.

He's concerned. "Stay away from those guys, man. Come to my house and hang out. You gotta stay away from the druggies, they're all screwed up."

How can I tell him that my friend is in a battle to keep his soul away from the devil? How can I explain that everything human within me longs to help him? In what manner can I possibly tell of the hopelessness of being unable to do ANYTHING? Oh the soul wrenching isolation of knowing evil in its darkest form; the fog thick and close. Unable to explain, I say nothing. My very being quivers under the crushing weight of the knowledge.

Toward evening I venture to John's house to spend the night. The 'ole farm auction is tomorrow so David and Rueben are in town as well. We hang out and talk like brothers do.

To compound my misery I sit and contemplate the family situation. Father is selling the farm because the boys are gone. I'm the one that should be at home. Glen has been left alone with the pressing load of the farm; now the family is forced to fold a losing hand. The guilt from years past presses on my heart. Despair and anger seep into me. Life is insane at the seams, and I'm caught in the middle. Through these past few years I've had many moments of pain and despair, but they never lasted long; always I pressed on, toughed it, partied it away. Now I can't get away from myself or from my life. The anguish is complete.

After a night of blessed escape I awake to a gray March day. Today is the end of an era; it is the family farm auction. Struggling up off the couch, I take my morning smoke. It's going to be a long day.

I chill with my brother Dave and his girlfriend Barb on the forty five minute drive to the farm. My brain calms a bit. The driveway is already choked with trucks and cars when we arrive.

The first person I encounter is my Dad. Wonder what's going through his mind. He greets me with surprise; the family didn't know I was in the area. Sauntering on into the house, I meet Mom and the girls. We watch the community folks gather out in the front yard; checking out the tables of household stuff and other junk, looking for a bargain. It is odd for me to see these old acquaintances again. They represent the days of my childhood, but my present reality is so far removed from the past that it feels like another lifetime entirely. My mind blazes on, struggling to adjust; struggling to find a solution for the question of evil...

The day fills with weird sounds and sensations as I wander from place to place. I am restless and not long in any one spot. Someone asks me about Ryan. A flood of emotions and pressure hammer the walls of my heart; I want understanding, a solution. Unable to voice the unspeakable, I say nothing.

A haunted feeling dogs me all day. Depressing thoughts bounce around my brain. My spirit is gripped in a vise and a voiceless scream sounds in my head, driving me up the wall. It feels as if my whole life has come to a head and I've messed it all up and am now fighting a hopeless battle with evil. The demons are right there, within my consciousness. But I hang out with the family and the relatives that showed up. It's enjoyable.

The pressure of the day has worn me down by late afternoon so I prepare to leave.

Confusion dances around me as I ease away and jump into my ride. I need to get high; very high. A few friends from out of state are around and the plans for later include chemicals and some herbal remedies designed to take away pain, physical or otherwise. We'll just have to see what a fat line of crank has to say about all this mental wretchedness. Sure haven't found anything else to ease the pain.

Later I hang with the guys, around a little music, a little smoke, a little powder. Ryan's around, wantin' a fix, wantin' some powder. Gotta have it, gotta quiet

The Odyssey of a Heart

these voices. Sorry pal. He's been awake far too long the way it is. We get high while he's not there. I can't enjoy myself. I snort the stuff, it burns like it always does, and my head slams into space. But there's a deep foreboding ache all the way down in my gut: what to do about Ryan? I tell my buddies the basic facts about the situation. The one understands; he knows all too well what's going on. Absolutely go to church, go tomorrow.

The 'ole pastor gets a call; gets a heads up about the spirits at work. "By all means come to church in the morning," he says. "We'll have a prayer service for you." He talks to Ryan, reassures him. And the pastor's got the power, for Ryan settles down to real sleep.

And the night crawls on, it flies on; it stops, it starts; it isn't, it is. The joints get passed around, the powder is laid out. Someone comes, someone goes. Talk floats around; talk and silence float around the tight little circle of friends. Got to keep that circle tight, can't let too many in. Too many people means trouble. Each one sits in an invisible cubicle, alternating between feeling bold, feeling alone, feeling stupid at the thought of some embarrassment from years ago. And the joint gets smoked - what's that outside the window there? That's daylight, buddy. It's morning.

With the breaking of day another guy shows up. "Pastor said you guys called him about Ryan. You need to go along. Be there by ten."

Go to church, me! I'm startled by this frightening thought. Sure I want to help Ryan, but my going to

The Odyssey of a Heart

church on this of all mornings wasn't exactly part of the plan. High as high can be, I ponder a way to escape my duty.

"Need to go home and clean up," I say. Maybe if I'm not around they'll go without me.

Back at John's house I announce to him I'm going to church. Mildly taken aback at the irony of the situation, he wishes me the best. In preparation to go, I smoke an enormous joint, inhaling to the furthest recesses of my lungs. The plain I'm on becomes higher, clearer. I am on my way to church; my body has more chemicals and THC in it than it has ever had before. The stage is set, the powers on high prepared to wrestle for the soul of man.

****

Time marches on. The wounds fester. The heart struggles to balance itself. Anger arises. Torment rages within.

Life is just life, and life hurts. The heart is tormented, but is either unwilling or unable to seek peace, to seek it hard. All the pain from over the years convinces it that this is just the way it is and must be. Peace is beyond reach; the void hangs hollow.

Sometimes the heart comes face to face with manifest evil. Having followed the destructive path of pain and isolation for years, it has reached a dark dungeon of lurking evil, the sheer horror of which bends and stretches the mind to its limit. The mind struggles to compensate, to find an answer. It works overtime, racing in a turbulent quest for stability.

The Odyssey of a Heart

The questions have no answers. One can not be prepared to deal with evil, solitaire. You can't know what it is until it's all around you, and then you're already engulfed by it.

With it, evil brings hopelessness beyond description. Faced with this incredible negative force, the heart becomes willing to reach beyond itself. Years of pain reside within and mix with the latest storm of insanity. Unable to press on, it seeks for something to still the inferno, for something to help.

My heart lies in a detached state as I drive toward the small town of Memphis, and my body and mind are almost incredibly stoned. Yet I am unable to remove myself from the reality of turmoil that swirls around me. The violently evil force that tortures Ryan is right there with me as well, bending and stretching my mind and forcing me to just shut it off the best I can. In addition, my spirit flirts with the unknown that lies within the church house doors. There also beams a tiny ray of hope; hope that in giving an insane situation over to church folks, something good might still happen.

As I climb out of the van in the church parking lot, all feeling is gone. The sun shines her warmth onto me; I shuffle across the gravel, unnoticing. Nature is grey and mechanical around me. The hills, the sky, the trees... they're all made of steel and concrete. The clear blue sky holds dark clouds, clouds of despair. With a few friends I step into the sanctuary where a special prayer service is set to begin. We sit close to the front, surrounded by maybe a dozen worshippers.

The service commences with a bit of piano and guitar, courtesy of the pastor and his wife. A slight feeling tugs at my heart, telling me that here are people who care, who might understand. Pain and turmoil inside my heart push the feeling aside. The last strains of piano die away as the pastor announces that today, prayer will be offered on the behalf of the visitors. Then without further ado he bows his head and addresses his Master in heaven. The assistant pastor also prays out loud, the rest of the congregation pleading with God either silently or very quietly.

This time of prayer affects me immediately. I feel I should bow my head as I have been taught, but the sheer strangeness of the situation keeps me from it. I just sit there in the pew with my head down, feeling something ever so slight rustling in my spirit.

Suddenly an incredible presence descends into the room; settles into the room and hovers around me. The very air is charged with a weight that presses inward with great power. The air is heavy enough to touch. And in my mind there rests not a shadow of a doubt that God Himself has entered the room. His presence far exceeds the physical presence of the people around me.

As soon as the presence of God reaches my senses; my reserves, yes, my walls, begin to unravel. Tears from the very depths of my soul push for exit as a great sorrow seizes upon me. The last few days have been spent in utter torture, and my spirit saw no hope. Now with the spirit of God pressing on me, the pressures inside push for release. I try to pray for Ryan, but can't seem to get through. Meanwhile my own sinfulness impresses my mind, but my flesh is too strong to give in. However, even with the personal agony I feel, my main concern is for Ryan. I see him glance about with a hunted look.

Soon I observe the pastor at the front of the church. His eyes are closed, his hands raised to the heavens, his voice lifted in supplication to the Presence that resides so strongly in the room. At that moment the spirit of God breaks through my walls, flooding me utterly; choking my throat and racking my body with great sobs as years of emotional lock-up burst forth. The overwhelming urge to give myself to God sears my soul with inviting warmth. The battle commences to rage.

The most immediate urge is to petition for my friend in such severe torment. My heart moves to reach God in prayer, instead it slams into a wall. I search the knowledge of the presence floating around me, and perceive I must give in to God before He can help me. However, all the lies I have believed for so long block my yearning for relief. My body is shaking with sobs I don't even try to contain. It feels right somehow. But my spirit resists the loving, peaceful call of God. I can't quite do it, I can't cross that line. What would I ever tell my friends? I want to pray for Ryan, not give my life to God.

The hellish forces struggle, fighting it out with the Spirit of light and peace. I hunch forward on the hard wooden pew, witness to the battle of battles, the battle within. The evil inside has come into the presence of the Risen Savior; something has to give. The thing inside screams for me to leave the building; it screams strongly, convincingly. My weeping intensifies as I realize I can not leave the building without interceding for Ryan. That alone keeps me inside the four walls.

I have come into the manifest presence of God, and divine knowledge impresses my very mind. It feels as if it has soaked right through my head. I realize there is evil within me, that I myself am a lost sinner, and that I can not much longer remain in the holy presence of God without giving in to the call. I decide I must go the distance.

And unseen force guides me from the pew to the front of the church. I kneel down by a little bench beside the pulpit. God and Satan do battle inside my heart as my spirit screams under the stress of this Great War. Lie after lie surface, but God helps me dismantle them all. The moment draws near as Satan whispers the lies I listened to as a young teen, the lies at the foundation of my personal deceit. But the presence of God is too strong, the falsehoods can not stand.

Finally my spirit simply breaks. Words are out of the question, but my heart speaks with God. "Here I am, Lord; I give myself totally to you. I will follow exactly what you tell me to do. Just help me. I'm tired of being afraid, lonely, angry, and hopeless. I want whatever it is you ask of me."

A monstrous weight - a physical weight! - lifts from my shoulders. A euphoric sense of freedom permeates my being. Joy explodes within my heart as the terrible torment of the last few days lifts from my soul. It is all right, God is in control.

I am free as a bird as I walk back to my seat, bowing my head in earnest prayer for my friend who has so intensely battled Satan these past weeks. My heart is at peace knowing that God hears and accepts my prayer.

After chatting briefly with the pastor and expressing my joy, I step out into the brilliant sunlight. The countryside lies in magnificent splendor as my spirit soars far beyond the confines of gravity. Nothing has really changed in my earthly circumstances, but I have hope as immense as heaven itself. Not a doubt, not a fear, not a temptation touch me as I commune with God. I am a new creature; Christ is in my heart.

Chapter eleven

The heart has met evil. Frantically it seeks within itself for something to counter this force. But the force is too great; of itself the heart can not win.

By the grace of God the heart is brought into the presence of Jesus. It immediately perceives that here is a power above all others. This is the Creator Himself.

Out of the gloom of despair hope is sighted. A shining peace calls softly. The heart almost dares hope; within the secret parts of itself, the heart almost dares to hope for an escape into a better world, a world of light and honesty.

The manifest presence of God accomplishes much. Its power soaks into the mind and reveals to it the true nature of God. A heart familiar with pain and resentment and torment will recognize the magic possibility of peace to be had, and commence to seek a way to attain it.

God's peace can be received in only one way: the heart must be willing to lay aside all its own desires, preferences, and grudges. It must desire to become a part, a follower of the source of this presence, this substance, this peace. It must want God more than any other thing or feeling. At the moment of surrender, the heart actually desires peace more than anything else. At this point God Himself enters the heart, bringing with Him vibrant peace and joy. In a sense He brings about a whole new heart. Before, the heart was struggling on under its own power. It followed what it thought best. It did what could be accomplished by itself. But now it turns to God, and God casts out the old and brings a power as mighty as heaven itself. HE is inside now; the heart is brand new. It has a fresh start, a new start, a new LIFE.

After having struggled to compensate for the great evil all around, the heart can now rest in the assurance of being within a power greater than all others. A good power. Outward things might not be changed, but from within emanates a brilliant joy. All this daunting stuff doesn't matter! God is in control! And so, the heart has now entered a peaceful realm where life still swirls about, but peace reigns inside. The heart is now in the embrace of timelessness, in the embrace of eternal timelessness in the arms of God.

The void is filled.

My maroon minivan eats up the road back to John's house as a perfect peace causes me to wonder in awe. There is PEACE in my heart. No torment! This is WILD. Never has anything been this real and never have I been so eager to share something with somebody. I must tell someone what happened to me. I can barely comprehend what has transpired but one thing I know: I have just been in the presence that created the universe and orders the seasons and gives me physical life.

John and Reuben are hanging out at the house when I arrive. In amazement they listen to the story I relate. Here they had seen me jacked up on meth on the way to church; now I gush forth with enthusiasm for God. Strange indeed. Candidly I describe to them the most profound experience of my life.

Fresh off the worst day of my life, I now savor the best one. Inside my heart the throbbing spirit of the Lord calms my soul and relaxes my mind. I have never known such peace. The worries and cares around me aren't even close to upsetting me. Jesus reigns.

Communing with my new best friend, I drive to Ryan's house as darkness lays hold of the Missouri hills. Something happened to him at church, and I surely do hope he got help for his heart and mind. Perhaps the voices have left him and he can regain some semblance of the peace he desperately needs.

Ryan looks changed somehow when I see him. His face still looks guarded but with maybe a hint of peace, and a hint of vagueness. We chat a bit before he wanders outside.

His girlfriend answers my questions. At church Ryan went to the front for prayer. A dozen members of the church gathered around him. An intense spiritual battled ensued. He thought God was telling him to leave the building. Meanwhile the prayer warriors called on God for intercession. Giving in, he allowed them to lay hands on him and pray. The Lord in His strength came through and the voices left his head, taking their torment with them. But Ryan is now in another difficult position. He had been listening to these many voices for some time. The voices shaped his reality but now they are gone. A great emptiness fills him and he doesn't know what to do or think.

Saying a few words of encouragement to him, I prepare to leave. I assure him of my prayers on his behalf. It is unsettling to see him still in a troubled state, but my peace remains.

Later that night one of my friends offers me a hit of meth. Arm outstretched, he holds a loaded light bulb. I readily refuse for I feel NO desire for chemicals. The peace in my heart is far better than any drugs I've ever taken.

The next week passes in a flurry of activity. I run into many people I grew up with. Folks call me on the phone. And every time, I tell them of the almost incredible joy in my heart. Without fear I testify to God's grace. Opening my mouth and speaking feels more important than anything else in the world.

On the third day of being a brand new man I cruise the roads in my van. Peace reigns and I am calm and happy. I listen to some music. Just like always, music for the road. Nirvana's strings and lyrics of the MTV Unplugged album float through the speakers. But this time their painful perspective slices through my joy and a gloom gathers round me. The sky grows a bit darker, an uneasy feeling steals into my heart. The music is not working.

I eject Cobain and insert a few other selections; music I absorbed while high on drugs. An hour later my outlook is murky, no longer am I happy. A wall has erected itself around me and imprisoned my mind. The unfiltered spirit of God has clashed with the thoughts and music of this world.

Suddenly a savage desire grips me. This music, while structurally superb, gives a message far from the peace and light that is God. I grab my CD collection and commence breaking the offending ones. Weakly they shatter into innumerable shreds.

When the last chip falls, about twenty albums are history. I feel spiritually strengthened for having rid myself of the music that clashed with the peace inside my heart. I am eager and willing to do anything to further God's kingdom.

Wanting to show an outward difference as well, I have my long hair cut that I had been growing in accordance with the alternative Rock style. Sporting my new look I visit my parents and tell them of God's rescuing of my heart and my subsequent turning to Him. Telling them brings us great joy.

My body still craves stimulants, however. By the next weekend I succumb to cravings and smoke a fat old joint. I feel great, floating away like always. I even talk with my cousin over the phone about my change of heart! But I sober up the next day and brother do I ever feel horrible. Smoking pot was obviously a mistake. It used to be an escape, now it grinds against my peace. Scolding myself harshly, I vow not to do it again.

The Odyssey of a Heart

It's time to head on back down to Carolina and get to work. On the way I stop over for about a week at Reuben's house and help work for a few days. One day the discussion at work turns to drugs; the evils of drugs specifically. But as I'm finding out, even after rejecting drugs there's still a tantalizing and morbid desire to talk about them. Maybe it's good and maybe it's not; it's just the way it is. So I relate my joy of being free of drugs even as a craving for cocaine steals into my body. Without really trying I'm feeling the fuzzy numbness in my nose and then I WANT it, bad. Problem is, I know where I can score some; I also know the danger of giving in.

We work and talk some more. I think about cocaine, I think about God, I think about the horror of the devil, I think about cocaine. It's quitting time and I think about cocaine. I give in to some sort of reasoning and jump into the truck with my buddy and head for the dealer. My mind races with reasoning and justifying. I ride shotgun and do battle up in my head and in my heart and in my very soul. We draw closer to our destination. It's only a few more miles. I think of what the Lord has done for me; the peace, the joy, the happiness. I know cocaine would wreck havoc into God's working in me. To fight or not to fight?...

We are almost there. The heaviness of the moment hangs on my soul. I remember the moment of surrender in the church house. I remember how liberating and empowering it was. "Keep driving, I can't do this," I hear myself say. We cruise away from the danger zone, victorious. We cruise away from a hell I might never escape if I enter into it once more.

It is past. I have survived my first bad craving for heavy drugs. The joy of the Lord returns in force. Peace springs from listening to God instead of the devil. God will take care of me. Ah… the joy of depending on a force greater that oneself.

Chapter twelve

I roll on back down to Carolina, across southern Indiana and down through Kentucky. Can't say I don't wish for a fat old joint to tide me over, but I don't have one. This is the first time in a long time I've traveled sober. An Interstate traffic jam adds four hours to the trip, I arrive around midnight, almost the same time I showed up here two months ago. This time my head is clear; no drugs involved.

And then comes Sunday. My co-worker Thomas got out of drugs lately, just like I did. Now he goes to church and I'm invited as well. So Nate and I go to a little Pentecostal joint for Sunday evening service. It's great; I'm thrilled to be in church. I've never been as sure about anything else as I am of one thing: this is right, this is good. Praise God!

So I get introduced to another small congregation. Guest speakers are two Harley riders, former drug dealing, gun packing roughnecks. Now they stand before us boldly speaking of the change God has wrought within them. Not what I'd grown up

The Odyssey of a Heart

with, though I doubt not a bit that God is glorified immensely by their testimony.

The days following are good. At work Thomas and I discuss Jesus and the power that is Him. My spirit rests.

But alas! My body remembers the buzz of marijuana. Kids I know still smoke it. Temptations tease me in weak moments. A week after arriving in SC, pot and I are in the same place at the same time and I just have to go and smoke a fat one. I can't even describe the pleasure it lends me. But four, five hours later as the THC wears off, my whole being hammers condemnation into my heart. I feel horrible. This is NOT working. Getting high takes my peace away. Far away.

From within whispers a voice of invitation. "Tell me about your troubles. Tell me how you feel. Repent. I will forgive."

It feels wrong; asking forgiveness for a sin I knew I shouldn't have done in the first place. I don't feel good enough to do it. But I feel bad about what I did, and ask God to pardon me. He grants His mercy wrapped in the embrace of peace.

The next few weeks hammer temptations into me at the times I am least equipped to handle them. I toke up a few times when the thought of never smoking marijuana again becomes too much to bear. I know it's wrong but I get around it and this thing grips me and I reason and rationalize. I convince myself it's OK, after which I light it up. After a few scenes like this followed by feeling terrible and repenting, the condemnation hits me as I smoke, and it doesn't leave. I get high and sit watching TV, all empty and miserable inside. I vow to never smoke again.

On a Saturday I journey up into North Carolina on a camping trip with about a half dozen college kids. Mountain bound, yea! We drive around hairpin curves and up steep grades and stare at the beauty around us. After two hours of travel we reach the trail head and hike about a mile down to a river and set up camp in a reasonably flat spot. We sit around and chat and soak in the wild nature around us. And someone breaks out a joint and it gets passed around. It comes to me and I reach for it and hold it between my thumb and index finger, put it to my mouth and draw it way back into my lungs. I know I shouldn't; I know it is wrong; but I do it anyway. I smoke the joint and I get high and that's that.

A little later a few of us hike down the river and get into the icy water. Out in the middle of the river I realize the guys plan to slide down over the twenty foot waterfall we are on top of. They sit on the rock and slide down over the edge with a splash into the pool below. I gotta go too, can't lose face now. All that marijuana in my system can't quiet the shock of the freezing water when I hit the pool. It takes my breath away for a good minute, sobering me up considerably.

Then it's back to camp and break out the food and the whiskey. Take a bite, take a drink, take a toke. Take a drink. I smother the voice of my conscience and get high and kinda tipsy on hard liquor. The river runs and darkness creeps over the mountains and a foreboding feeling of mystery settles into my gut.

A presence lurks outside the ring of the campfire, a presence of uneasiness. We stroll back down to the small falls and sit in the dark, watching the river run strong. A vastness sweeps me up and I am in something, something big and frightening and terrible; yet warm and inviting. We hike further down the river to the big falls, where the water drops a hundred feet. We sit right at the top as the cool wind drafts off the rushing water and blows around my head. The presence grows stronger and a feeling pulls at my mind, pulls me to the lip of the falls, but I sit on the rock, unable to move. The vastness takes on the thrill of challenging God and right then I know it's evil. As the force shows me the edge of the cliff a voice sounds in my brain, loudly and clearly, "The devil's here, the devil's here, the devil's here, the devil's here." Faster and faster and faster and faster and louder it shouts in my ear and I focus my mind and talk to it and try to calm it. Louder and louder and louder and shriller. I focus and zone and calm myself. And then someone makes a move to go back to camp and I walk away from the edge and back into the light of the fire.

Late at night I get some sleep before awakening to a clear morning and breakfast frying over the campfire. I am not getting high today no matter how many joints get handed to me. What I did last night was wrong and I feel terrible. Somehow I was in the presence of evil and I am still okay. My heart bleeds with regret. I want to get back home so I can go to church tonight with Thomas. I want church, I want God.

We make it back to town late in the afternoon. My soul longs for communion with God but I feel small and worthless. Still I tell Him of my wrongs and ask forgiveness. It doesn't feel like I am forgiven or righteous. But I'm truly sorry. Surely God has forgiven me?

I drive to church as the tears fall from my eyes. The quietness of God steals into my soul; a peace takes hold. I meet Thomas in the parking lot and we talk for a few minutes. He sees my red eyes and asks, "You been getting high?" I don't want to admit it but this is Thomas, he understands. So I tell him about it.

"Lean on God and ask for the strength to resist the cravings," he says. "Nothing else will work."

We walk into the church house, brothers at heart. We both need God daily to stay clean, to stay right.

I hit the job Monday morning with my conscience clear and the hope of God abiding in my chest.

I need to make a break from this environment. It's too easy to get weed and I'm often around stoners. Perhaps I could go back to the Amish way in Worthington, Indiana where a bunch of my relatives are. Hmm, that might be just the thing. If I would make such a radical move it would about have to help me on the spiritual front. Just doing something openly for the better carries power, I have found. I smashed my CD collection, did I not? I know moving would be the right thing to do, but I can't quite bring myself to just let go and do it. I know the protection of brotherhood is precisely what I need. But I guess I don't want the blessings badly enough.

The Odyssey of a Heart

A few more weeks go by. I get high a few more times. I get miserable a few more times, and I seek forgiveness a few more times. When I get high and I'm feeling guilty, I'm afraid to talk with God, so I hide behind the cover of absence. But Thomas checks up on me, he guards my heart when I am too weak to do so. After a period of days of my not praying to God or reading the Bible, Thomas and I cruise town one night and talk for a long time. Discouraged, I just don't know if it's worth it; I don't know if I can go on. But Thomas argues the case for God. "Just ask forgiveness when you sin. Do anything you can to not sin. Focus on God. God is powerful, He can help you. It's worth it, just let go and hold on to Jesus. He gave His blood for you, man."

Verily, Thomas pulls me back from the edge. I go home with hope in my heart.

And I go to church and rejoice in the mercies of God. He is giving me every chance in the world to get away from the addictions that ensnare me. He pours forth His spirit without measure.

One night I cruise home from a visit to the local college campus. The buzzing effects of marijuana grip my body. Driving west on a back road, I glance up at the blood red moon in front and to the left of me. Memories of road trips on meth crash land into my brain as that feeling of timelessness teases my body. A craving as big as the universe itself floods me with an aching need to get numb with chemicals. Evil lurks around me, and the devil is calling with a deal, right out on the table where we can all see it: I enjoy the hypnotic highs of hard drugs for life

The Odyssey of a Heart

if I but give up all that I now have. My peace with God would be gone and I'd always have to live with the pain of having let my family and friends down. I could do exactly what I pleased.

Driving down the highway, it doesn't seem like that bad a deal.

In the light of day the spirit of darkness I wrestle with at night seems too strange to be real. But it is real. I need to tell someone about it. I need to take it to God, but I feel so alone when I don't tell a human as well.

God calls me to move to Indiana. I know this move to be highly beneficial; it would cut off my easy access to drugs. But I resist the step, not wanting to make such a radical lifestyle change. My denial slowly gnaws at my peace even as I try to block it out.

One day I discover I have a hernia and will have to get it sewed up. This financial and physical hurdle hits me hard with uncertainty and depression. In fact, I drive right home from the meeting with the doctor, get some weed delivered to me, and get high. I don't know why this had to happen now or what the meaning of it is. It doesn't feel right to just get high, but that's the quickest way to ease my anxieties.

After Nate harasses the doctor and gets him to move the surgery up a few days, I have to wait only three days instead of six. I am trucked back home in severe pain the same evening, a pain mostly dulled by good legal drugs. I eat so many pills in the first twenty four hours after surgery that my stomach commences hurting worse than my wound. My mind

The Odyssey of a Heart

is way out there, bouncing to and fro in the atmosphere that is unmistakably medical drugs. What I need to do is stop taking them. So I smoke pot. I simply need a pain killer.

A few days later Nate leaves to attend a family funeral, and I am at the house alone. I get one visitor the first day. So here I am; all alone, strung out, unable to drive, hurting, and plain depressed. I rise a bit before noon, after which I smoke a joint and watch TV all afternoon. I am lonely upon lonely. I sit on the easy chair, my body idle and my mind trying to stay strong. Down, down, down.

The next day drags from its birth onward. My heart speaks to no one, God or man. I am very alone.

I smoke some weed.

I watch TV.

This crawls on into the third day. The hours drag by, the emptiness within is almost physically unbearable on top of the mental strain it carries. It is the emptiness of resisting God. Finally my soul can take no more, and my knees bend before God. I cry out, "O Lord, I know I'm doing wrong. I'm smoking pot and not even praying to you. I'm sorry. I'll now do what ever you want me to. I WANT to do your will. Anything Lord."

Weeping, I kneel in the holy presence of God. The sweet echo of surrender plays in my mind. I have grown so miserable that now I just want to do God's will. I want peace. It seems I should go to the church at Worthington. Well, that's what I'll do. I'll go the distance.

I call a few folks and confirm that I'm moving to Indiana. I need to let others know, else I might not go through with it.

O the long journey back to the conservative ways of life! How can I ever do it? I had considered myself permanently out of the culture of my childhood. How will it be?

Life is to me a black and white existence. There is good; there is evil. These two facts envelop my complete being. I myself am powerless against evil. My only hope is to gain help from a force stronger than myself; something stronger than evil. That something is God. If God wants me to take a course of action, I'm willing to take it. So I aim my sights on a culture of seclusion.

Loading my mini van with my meager collection of earthly belongings, I head for the Midwest. I stop to visit my brothers in Illinois for a few days. I get rid of a few modern conveniences. My mind is slightly dazed for the radical changes that are taking place. But if God is for me, who can be against me?

Brother Rueben drives me to Worthington in his Dodge truck. It feels crazy to do what I'm doing, like I'm cutting a safety line and plunging into a place of no escape. This is some major stuff, my friend. We draw near to my new home, a renting situation where I'll be staying with family.

And then, here we are. We unload my stuff into my room and drink some coffee and share some chit chat with my uncle. After an hour Reuben prepares to leave and I bravely bid him farewell. He and his truck are the last signs of my independent American lifestyle that I can still see, and those are about to disappear. But, I remember the feeling of peace and surrender to God; and this is what He wants. So be it.

Reuben pulls out of sight, up the road and gone. The tailgate disappearing around the bend slams reality full into my face. It's done. My world has just taken a plunge from a cliff; the landing statistics are uncertain at best.

My former experience with church life wasn't the best. Rebellion played a part early. I was a bad guy. In turn the church took the counter measures they saw necessary. I strongly resented their handling of the youth in general. Leaving home at sixteen, I lived exactly the way I wanted. After returning home and leaving a few times, I was gone for good. Falling into a world of drugs, I ended up in trouble with the law. My drug use only escalated. Living life on the edge, I came face to face with evil. As I plunged to the depths of the pit of darkness I cried out to the Living God. Surrendering my will to His, I was given a new heart through the blood of His son Jesus Christ. With the memory of my heavenly encounter burning in my soul, I set out to live my life for Him. But alas, I am still trapped in my earthly body, some of my addictions wanting satisfaction. Now I seek to lead my life in a place set apart from easy access to the things my flesh most desires.

Now that I am in Worthington, I continue going to weekly worship services with an occasional Bible

The Odyssey of a Heart

Study mixed in. Where I had been getting a daily dose of liberal ideology from modern music, I am now being fed the nourishing richness of God's Living Word. Concerned brethren support me, asking how I'm holding up under the spiritual battles. The youth include me in their activities.

I slowly thaw to the warmth of brotherhood fellowship.

And I fight a constant urge to get high. A powerful feeling pulls on me most of the day, every day. I counter by immersing myself in God's Word. Scripture verses occupy my mind. Spiritual books give encouragement as do the discussions with others. But always the urges return.

Many people pray for me that I might remain victorious. Friends stay in touch and my brothers are always there. But my battle is private; the demons of addiction are felt by me alone. The thoughts come to my head; other folks can't see them. It forces me to go to God constantly. Negligence means defeat. The stakes are as high as heaven itself. My eyes can only look to one place, which is Jesus.

The spiritual food I get at church and Bible Study prove cleansing for my soul. Joy and peace abound without measure. God is REAL. All around is the evidence of Him.

The flesh lies in wait....

During the day I am beset with cravings for meth. This I can handle; it is just a strain on my coping abilities. But during the night the real terror begins. Dreams invade my sleep. Sometimes I am in a lonely room with a line of crank before me. I go down, snort

The Odyssey of a Heart

it, and drift away knowing I shouldn't have done it. A wretched condemned feeling burns in my soul. Then suddenly I'm awake again.

After another day of joy, then craving; my head is on the pillow once more. I drift away as evil visions bombard me. I am running through the woods with army tanks chasing me close behind. Running up a lonely hill, I see an abandoned shack. I don't want to die, I want to live. I need to get out of sight. Desperate, I lunge toward the shack, the growl of the tanks sounding in my ear. The guns are back there. Pounding the last few yards to the door, I leap inside, out of sight of the enemy. I peer out the dusty window; the tanks roll on up the hill, the gaping hollow of gun muzzles staring at me. But something is wrong here inside as well. A feeling of a presence pricks my consciousness. Slowly I turn to look around the dusty room for the first time. The floor is covered with skeletons, intact. Aghast, I watch as they slowly move, then rise from the floor. They stare at me with a bony gaze, they move my way... Terrified, I awake.

The dreams continue for weeks. I've made a commitment to God, and the devil is furious. He wants me back. At least he won't give up this round without an all out slugfest. So I get the cravings during the day and the nightmares after dark. God is always somewhere close, hanging around waiting for the calls for help. I plead with Him to end the mental tortures. But in His wisdom He allows them to continue.

The Lord is getting a stronger hold on my life and Satan is desperate. The night time terrors switch to actual visions. Falling asleep is the worst time. I lie in bed, staving off sleep, wanting to stay in control, to guard my mind; but I drift away anyway. Almost into the land of oblivion, and I go into a wild rushing fall- straight down, my body rushing a thousand miles per hour. Every ounce of my being is electrified, gripped in a terrifying power. Evil jabs me from all sides. I try to move, to snap out of it. Desperately I will my finger to twitch, just a wee tiny bit. Bam, I'm out of it. I've stopped. I'm awake. I've never even fallen asleep.

The pattern continues on other nights. I know what the enemy is doing. He wants to give up no more ground to the power of Light. He hammers away at my mind with the power of evil. My only way of dealing with it is to turn wholly to God. The Lord always delivers. Joy and peace are a daily part of my life. And the horrors of night time keep me in close contact with God.

I continue studying the Bible. More tools for overcoming temptation join my arsenal. The enemy struggles harder. He wants me on drugs. Lies float into my ears, telling of the incredible wonders of chemical drugs.

My subconscious visions reach a climax. I am afraid to go to bed at night, knowing full well the terror to come. One night I lie in bed, drifting away. A savage rush rips my body. I'm still awake and even able to see the moonlight outside. Falling, I see a black monster towering over me. Frantically I try to move. I'm in a free fall, down, down, down. Snap, and I'm good. But I can't get away. I can see out the window, but I'm powerless to stand or sit up. Here we go again. I'm rushing downward; I can't move. The monster bends over me, reaches down... A voiceless scream tears at my throat. Pure horror forces me to move my muscles, and I snap out of it. Finally being able to move, I sit up in bed. Evil floats around me.

I survive such incidents only with God's help. His comforting presence is never far away. As I lean more heavily on Him, the enemy's attacks become weaker. The last time I see the monster, he is almost white. I am at John's house and happen to sleep in the room where I got stoned all the time in the old days. The powers fight it out there on my old turf. In the early morning hours, the monster hovers over my bed, but his powers of terror are gone. The blackness has faded from his being. I awake and know he is gone for good. My cravings become almost a thing of the past. And the Lord, blessed be His name, is ever close by.

Chapter thirteen

The summer of '01. What a good time to be young and free. I travel here and there; for a week, for a weekend. I love hitting the road or the rail and racing toward my destination. Most of the time. The drug charges are for some reason resurrected from the Scotland County archives; consequently, the law forces me to travel to Missouri. Unfortunately John is dragged into the mess as well since my drugs were found at his house. The drug bust just won't go away. I go to Missouri and meet my lawyer, give him some more money, and look to him for a bit of reassurance. I'm sure he has many talents, but putting his clients at ease isn't one of them. So I enter the courtroom with my nerves hopping, not knowing what awaits me.

Well, it seems the first order of business is to sit in here for a while so my attorney can rack up some hours. My case "State of Missouri versus Mervin Wagler" comes to the docket and I tremble a bit. What did I ever do against the state of Missouri?

Apparently the judge thinks it was something worth noting, for here I am. Anyway, my lawyer requests a stay or an extension or an inquiry or something like that. It's granted and I am ordered to return in thirty days at 9am sharp.

I go back to Indiana and hire myself onto a log home construction crew. Now I get to carry heavy logs and work on ruining my back. It is hard work with moderate pay, but it is good to be working. Structure, man. This construction crew has a good sense of humor and wit, much like every crew I've ever worked on. I feel lucky for my position. Hey, not everyone gets to work with a guy that raises snakes and rats. And I get to work with one of my uncles, John, as well. We talk and laugh about life and about family. He asks me how my heart is doing, how I'm holding up under the pressure of battle. I can talk to him, man to man. He's cool.

With logs on my shoulder and sweat on my brow, I think about my legal troubles. I know I'm not going to the gallows or even to prison, but I might be going to jail. I tell myself that it isn't a big deal. Maybe it isn't. But I think about it a lot. I feel anger at the police that came and besieged my house without good cause. Coming home to the sight of a bunch of law officers going through your stuff is hard to stomach; that feeling of violation grinds me even now. I feel angry toward the hospital worker that I believe gave me up to the law. Oh well.

I go back to Missouri with a knot in my chest, go to court and listen to the legal speak. His honor hems and haws and schedules another appearance for next month. Just push the verdict on out there, ole' judge. I know I'm just another number to you, just another case. It doesn't matter to you how I feel; just another day on the job. But this is big stuff to me, your honor. This is my life. You hold a portion of my future there in your file. Take it seriously.

And I go out to see the family. I'm upset because of the court appearance I just came from, and I sit moodily in the house. Mom sits in her office and makes greeting cards and Mary works in the kitchen and seven year old Samuel reads a book, and they steal glances at me, the sullen, silent one. My spirit moves restlessly within me for no good reason, but I can't do anything about it. I wander out to the back pasture and walk down the fence row a ways. I sit and stare at the sky and try to reach God. The uncertainty of my future presses upon me and I allow the tears to fall, and God speaks peace to my soul. I go to him as best I can and the peace comes quietly. I return to the house with a song on my lips and chat with the girls, and we drink coffee and eat fresh baked chocolate chip cookies.

Back in Worthington I work on keeping it cool. The Bible Studies prove to be a channel for God's truth to enter and strengthen my heart and mind. We youth are able to present our questions and discuss the problems we struggle with and the joys we share. It's all pretty much black and white. I don't think of dope much. Instead I partake of the natural pleasures of life.

Behind the house stands a heavy forest filled with ravines, trees, and rocks. After work I'm often out back climbing hills, examining plants, stalking wild game; anything the old woods has to offer. This atmosphere calms and soothes my soul. Here I see intricate detail, constructed by a Master designer. If God cares about making a tiny insect to survive in the woods, he must care about me.

I ride my bike in the meadows and through the woods; up the dirt path, all focus and screaming muscles. At the top it is breathe, feel your heart pound, crouch on the pedals and rage down the hill. And only use the brakes long after you need them. Airtime, that's what I want; an awesome thrill, without the chemicals.

And the days hammer away and the grasses grow as the sun shines hot on southern Indiana. I study the Bible diligently and the seeds my parents planted in my heart years ago sprout slowly. The grace of God stays constantly on the fringes of my mind. And I rise at 4:30am and travel two and a half hours to work so I can carry heavy logs and make a little money, a little money to fund my next trip to court.

I hear from my lawyer that the prosecutor might be ready to cut a deal. What this means I don't know. Perhaps the law has no case after all? Maybe I should fight it all the way. But if I accept a deal, I'll know what I'm getting. With these thoughts I roll on back out to good old Missouri where the judge awaits me and my criminal past. But first I chat with the lawyer and get the latest. I can cut a deal that gives me thirty days in jail, five years probation, and two hundred hours of community service. These are not exactly attractive figures, but they make sense for two reasons: if I accept the conditions, John's name will be cleared and I will not be convicted of a felony.

So I enter the courtroom again and accomplish I'm not sure what, but I'm sure welcome to come back in thirty days and plead guilty to my crimes. More precisely, I must return and I may plead if I so desire. Same old, same old.

Slowly the legal pendulum swings, unnervingly so.

The tension grows. Going before the judge and admitting my crimes feels like a dangerous thing to do. But I don't want to fight it and risk a bunch of jail time and the brand of felon for my whole life. The months of summer have slipped away and we approach fall and somehow I land a job in a cabinet shop. This means I run a table saw and try not to cut off my fingers, it also means I work in the midst of my brethren. They try to keep me built up through these trying times. Another court appearance draws nigh.

On the fateful day of confession, I meet early with my attorney in a little room off to the side. He states that we will plead guilty today, and I grill him once more on the specifics of the plea bargain. I sure don't want to give them evidence they can use against me if we do for some reason go all the way to trial.

The judge sits up high, front and center. I sit on one of the benches close to the front. Funny how similar these seats are to church pews. A case gets called and the judge rules. Another case is processed. Then, the judge declares it is time to process "State of Missouri versus Mervin Wagler".

What is this? The judge is looking at me. Stand right up here he says. Confused, I shuffle up to the clerk or the recorder or whatever. I look at my attorney, wondering what in the world is going on. Apparently he missed telling me few important details. Do what? Yes, I swear to tell the truth, the whole truth, and nothing but the truth, so help me God. You may sit down right over here. Up here. It's the witness stand.

I climb into the witness stand as my heart pounds in my chest. I'm going to testify against myself in open court, but I have no idea what to say. Why wasn't I briefed on this proceeding? How worthless could a lawyer be? I look at him, imploring him to do something. But the judge is speaking.

Were the marijuana pipes yours? Yes sir, all mine. What about the meth hitter and the meth that was found. Mine, your honor. Where were these items found? They were in my house, sir. Were you aware that they were there and also, were you aware of their illegal nature? Yes, your honor, I was fully aware they were there and that they were illegal. Thank you, you may step down. Your sentencing is set for November seven, 2001, at 9am.

Thanks a lot, old boy.

It is slightly ridiculous pleading to possession of meth when the only meth found was the residue inside the pipe. But friend, there's no turning back now. At least I know when I will be sentenced, and then I'll know what my fate will be. November 7. I've got a full month to deal with that.

The Odyssey of a Heart

With much trepidation I await the sentencing. The unknown bothers me. Going to jail isn't that big a deal and probation can be dealt with. But no knowing what will happen drives me crazy. I guess it gives me a good chance to just say, "Hey God, this is what it's all about, right? I don't know what the future holds, but You do. So if I can relax and trust You, it will all be alright." Such thoughts bring peace; any negative possibilities are of little consequence. Most of the time.

October hurries away and all too soon it is time to travel once more. I've grown to like my work at the shop, the responsibility of accomplishing a task on my own. I also like the connection I feel to the guys I work with every day. There's also a connection and a support from the community in general; to wit, my grandparents and the folks I stay with accompany me out to Missouri. They've got my back.

First of all, we go to my parent's house in Iowa. We hang out and it's all good. But tomorrow hangs over my head. I sleep reasonably well and awake with that strung out, nervous feeling. This sucks. But my parents are there for me; they'll go along too. I've got a regular army looking out for me.

On the forty five minute drive down across the state line, we don't talk much. We sit and we think. After a while we break out a few hymns to sing. I know not what awaits me, but I will sing. I have broken the law and I will be punished, but I've got a lot to sing about.

Amazing grace, how sweet the sound,
That saved a wretch like me.

The Odyssey of a Heart

I once was lost but now I'm found,
Was blind but now I see…
The memories roll, and the tears roll.

I enter the courtroom the recipient of more support than anyone else present. And we sit on some benches and we think. We ponder. 9am comes and court is in session; 9am goes and my lawyer is nowhere to be seen. The cases are called and processed. Up front sits a prisoner in blaze orange, getting his day in court. Perhaps I'll get to meet him later.

A half hour rolls by. A young man about my age requests and is granted a change of his last name. The cases are presented and processed. The minutes roll by and my attorney finally shows himself, close to ten o'clock.

This time I meet with my lawyer in the little room as the leader of a half dozen supporters. They listen soberly as the wise one explains the probable outcome of the sentencing. Jail time, people; that's what we're looking at.

Back out into the court room and the state of Missouri can finally have her say about me. The judge painstakingly goes over pages of paperwork, rehashing the particulars. My sins are laid bare for the people to see.

And the judge's gavel falls.

You, Mervin Wagler, are hereby sentenced to thirty days shock detention in the Scotland county jail, five years probation, and two hundred hours of community service. You need to speak to the probation official over there, and you are now under the charge of deputy Hollins.

The Odyssey of a Heart

Thanks a lot, judge. Good job.

And just like that, I am a prisoner. I can no longer come and go as I please.

I get to speak with my supporters and try to reassure them that I'm OK. With hugs and tears, they have nothing left to do but go.

As they leave the courtroom, I remember something I need to tell my dad. So I just go ahead and step outside the room into the hall and say a few words. A very excited deputy rushes out the door in search of me, not wanting such a fresh prisoner to escape his clutches so quickly.

I sit back inside and wait on my new superiors. The blaze orange guy gets set free from jail but saddled with probation. "You get to take my place now," he chuckles as he shuffles past me, out of the courtroom and onto the street. And I sit and ponder my new status as prisoner, my status as the newest resident of a small room in the back of the basement of the county courthouse. Funds must be tight, for that is what the jail consists of here in Hicktown, USA.

When I finally get downstairs to the cop shop, the processing begins in earnest. We need information: fingerprints, address, and social security. And I wait and think. On the wall hang a few TV monitors with their eyes on the inmates. There they are; my new friends. I watch the black and white images, wondering how it will be, how jail life is. Actually, I'm not as nervous as I was before the judge read my sentence to me.

I'm a prisoner of the state.

And since I'm a prisoner, I do what I'm told. The deputy and I march across the hall to the storage room where all kinds of clutter abide, including much blaze orange clothing, tiny portions of soap and deodorant and other prisoner necessities, and a large plastic marijuana plant. I place my stuff in two small gray tubs, one for in the cell and one for storage in this room. Nothing dangerous may find its way behind the bars, which means I must leave my little tablet with its wire spiral here in storage; otherwise, I might strangle someone with it.

And the time is here. I walk with my escort down the hall, down the hall toward the steel door with a little mesh window. The door clangs open and we step into *the room*. There is a narrow aisle at the front, this side of the bars. It is interesting that I would have to break down two doors to escape; it sure doesn't look like I'll be able to get through the small window cut out of the back wall there. It is covered with a web of one inch rebar. There are three cells along the wall on the left with what looks like two beds in each one. The other two third of the jail is one room with a big picnic table in the middle of it. A guy lounges on his cruel looking iron bed and three more guys sit at the table where the ancient TV crackles away. They all look.

The key slides into the lock, it turns to the left, and the bolt slides free and the inmates watch. The door swings out toward me and the way is clear. Clutching my tiny gray basket of essentials, I step on in and walk back toward an empty cell.

"What are you in here for?" asks a middle aged guy.

"Possession of meth."

"Bleeping druggie."

He's cool. And it does look like he might be intimately familiar with meth and the possession thereof.

And the door clangs shut behind me and the key is inserted and turned. I am locked in a smelly grey room at the bottom of the courthouse. I walk on back toward the window and peer out. Bummer; there's barely any daylight visible. The window is set down into the ground. There's even a shower in here. Nice. And the toilet- let's just say there won't be a lot of privacy.

Into the cell I go and look for my corner. The cell is all mine. This brings up a difficult choice: there are two 'beds'. Which is best, the iron pallet up top or the one on bottom?

Once again I do what I do best of late: I sit and think. I sit on the thin mattress, dressed in my blaze orange, baggy suit, and I look around my cell. On the wall are signs of the passage of other humans. There is a bit of graffiti and heartbreakingly, a large amount of days counted off by tiny scratch marks in groups of five. Looks like someone anticipating the day of freedom, or prison. Everything is painted gray.

I'm in jail; the door is locked. The room is small and musty.

Chapter fourteen

The walls, they make a hollow sound,
The walls!
The doors, they bang a hollow sound,
The doors!
The bars, they hold me in my cell,
The bars!
The walls! The doors! The bars!
The walls!

The TV runs on endless shows and the lights struggle to brighten the dim, musty room. The prisoners lounge around, being lazy because there is nothing else to do. The bars stare vacantly inward and the walls stand solid and confining. The glass of the window strains to see daylight but it is still happy if it can't, for it is well protected by heavy iron bars from the inmates inside. The concrete floor lays unmoving and solid. The heavy ceiling hangs overhead and completes the cage that holds these idle men captive, the men that were created with freedom of choice and love for freedom, a NEED for freedom. And they've got freedom. They possess the freedom to think about the outside, about driving down the road, and about hanging out with friends. The freedom to roll out of bed at six in the morning and grab the tray of food the jailor shoves through the slot in the door, and to eat it if the stomach feels strong. And early in the morning is the best time to eat, for the food gets real nasty the next two meals of the day. The food is bad but you are locked up, so there's not much you can do about it. But if you get tired of it you can holler till the deputy comes to talk, you can threaten to throw the nasty food on him; and if you are really fed up you charge the bars with the slimy stuff and throw it out into the main hall. You're in jail, man. You are locked up in a cage. You can think about it and stress about it; you can let the walls close in, you can go nuts; but there's nothing you can do to change it. Your heart is lonely within your chest and your mind wanders and you want to wander; you want to wander outside these walls, for crying out loud.

So, I'm in jail. I'm lucky to have a work release after seven days. But for seven days and nights I won't be able to leave this pen. I'll have to sit here in a cage and just be here. There is no escape. Would there be a fire, we would be totally at the mercy of others to help us. I'm here. Right here. Only here.

It's only the first evening and I'm already feeling cut off from the world. Time is losing meaning before my very eyes. There is activity, free will activity moving all around us inmates; it's happening on the outside, on the outside of this pocket of the timelessness of jail. The world moves, but we do not.

At six o'clock the jailor delivers a plate of food for each prisoner. Supposedly the food comes from a local restaurant; we're not sure where it comes from, what we do know is that it is not good.

We eat our humble meal and watch TV, and the guys answer my questions about the procedures of the jailhouse routine. It's pretty basic: three meals a day, fifteen minutes of visiting a week if someone comes to see you, laundry once a week, and a Sunday morning visit from the pastor. We have a phone we can call out on, collect; and we may receive mail. TV and lights off at eleven each night.

And that's about it. Not much going on in here.

Two of the kids in here are younger than I. They are both on their way back to minimum security prison, both on drug related charges. One of them went to the joint the first time for drugs and then got out early, but he was saddled with an ankle bracelet. One day as he sat in his house he got tired of wearing the thing so he took a pair of bolt cutters and cut it off. Ten minutes later he was calmly smoking a cigarette when the police came to get him. Now here he is, on the way back in for another two years. And the older ones are also on the way back in. It sounds like they escaped from a half way house and commenced cooking meth and (shock, shock) got caught and are headed back in for ten year stretches. Hey, come to think of it, we are all in here on drug related charges.

The Odyssey of a Heart

I spend a restless night on the uncomfortable bed. But I sleep. I don't have to worry about the guys in here; they are not out to hurt me. Actually, they are very friendly and helpful. I sleep and dream some dreams, the ones you can't quite get a handle on. Then in the quiet sleep before dawn the door rattles and the jailor hollers 'breakfast' and it's time to roll out of bed if I want to eat.

Four of us roll out of bed and eat, all groggy eyed and tired. The food is pretty good actually; eggs, bacon, toast, and a bit of potato. So we gobble down the food, watch the news a bit, and climb back into bed. We don't have to get up! We can stay in bed as long as we want. So I sleep for a while. Upon awakening my new reality bombs my mind again. I pray to God and read the Bible, and I arise from bed and amble out to the picnic table, the social center of our world here. Don't want to stay in bed too long. In here you need to have some focus, something to do. I don't want to lie in bed in the morning because I'M **TRAPPED** IN HERE!!! I can't get out. If I just lie there I feel trapped, but if I get up and move around and talk or write or walk around and exercise, then I'm taking control of myself. I'm using freedom of choice. Freedom.

And the day ticks on by. Nothing happens. We sit. Sometimes we talk. Every once in a while someone walks around, getting a drink, going through his stuff, or just moving around. There is a very basic, almost childlike atmosphere among the guys. The small things are important; the small things make a guy 'happy'. You are 'set up' if you have *stuff*. Things like color pens, nice paper, a normal shirt, kool aid mix, etc. Along the same line, the guys are free of most petty instincts, they are straight up. They've got each other's back.

The meals come at the appointed times and we pick at the food. It's low quality. I decide to fast for a few days in hopes of committing my jail stay to God and gaining control of my spirit. This is time that the Lord can use to his honor and glory, but only if I stay tuned in to him. So I'll fast and the other guys will get to pick at my food in addition to theirs.

And the night comes and I lie in my cell and try to commune with God. In a way I feel close to Him, maybe because I feel close to the inmates. I'm inside this pen; I'm inside here with other unfortunates. We are on the same page. Time moves swiftly during the night as the guys sit at the table and talk about drugs and I lie on my cot and talk to myself and God. The loss of my freedom bears down on my mind stronger and stronger. I commence thinking about many little things I took for granted on the outside; about the little things that make **freedom** great.

I sleep restlessly.

CLANG, CLANG!! "Breakfast," hollers the jailor. It's 6am.

And another day begins. I lie in bed because I have renounced food for the next few days. No pressing duties await me today here in the county jail. Perhaps I'll call someone later. That sounds like a pretty major project. But first I will be quiet in my spirit and commune with God, and look for strength for the day. And I need strength. I'm tough and the guys are friendly, but I am essentially cut off from my whole network of family and friends. I can call if I want to, and after a few days I might receive some mail, but for now the line has been cut. It's cool, I can handle it. But still… a knot forms in my throat when I think of all *my people* on the outside. I long to be with my family and my brethren. There is a certain isolation peculiar to a jail cell.

Wait a minute. Today is Friday, visiting day. I get my fifteen minutes out of the cell if I do in fact receive visitors. Hope someone shows.

The day rolls on by with a mix of meditation, prayer, and conversation. The guys are easy to talk to. They have seen the hard edge of life and are stripped of the layers of reserve that so often hamper real communication in normal social situations. The big issue of imprisonment looms large and unyielding and almost unapproachable; thereby, each prisoner releases the layers of social reserve and focuses on the real things in life: food, water, comfort, and a bond with their fellowman.

In the afternoon the jailor comes on back to the cell and unlocks the hated door, and orders me to follow him. I saunter out into the aisle and follow, shuffling along with my jail issue flip flops and clad in my blaze orange clothes. On we go into a tiny room and here are my mother and John and Reuben and a few of the younger ones. Familiar faces! I am well at ease and we talk and laugh for but a moment and the fifteen minutes are up. And that's it.

The day fades away and the night steals quietly over the land and into the jail room, hovering restlessly outside the sliver of the window on the wall. Night time passes faster than the daylight hours, so we sit up late and watch TV and talk. At 11 o'clock the power is shut off, taking the lights and the TV along. Then we just talk.

The talk is about drugs. My fellow inmates like drugs, man; they like them a lot. I like them too, but I don't use them anymore. I try not to think about drugs either, but the truth of the matter is that I like to smoke pot and snort meth and trip on acid. I hope I never do that stuff again, but I know I would enjoy the rush. So we are all united in our appreciation for mind altering substances. The talk dwells on the consumption of drugs, their availability, their quality; and the growing of pot and the manufacturing of meth.

"I will do meth until the day I die," declares the senior inmate.

He will likely do just that.

The night floats on and I doze on my iron pallet of a bed. Food arrives at 6am sharp but I stay away from it. I am becoming quite hungry, so I try to focus my mind on God. The Bible beckons me to exploration; to the contemplation of the things of God. My 'self' calls me to watch TV and talk about neutral things with the guys. There might not be anything wrong with that, but zoning in on God is the better choice.

I read scripture, pray, and think about my family. Quietly I sing a few hymns. After a while I realize this is Sunday, and I pray for the sermons being prepared and given in churches throughout our land. About nine o'clock the outside door creaks open and the

The Odyssey of a Heart

pastor from my favorite church walks in, the pastor who called down God's spirit on me the day of my great change. Boy, am I ever glad to see him. His wife is also along and we chat for a bit. He gives us some encouragement and scripture reading, and then breaks out a guitar and they sing a few hymns. He promises to be back in a week and tells us to call him if we need anything or just want to talk.

May the Lord richly bless this faithful servant. 'I was in prison and he visited me.'

The hours tick away. A deputy shows up with an unkempt brute of a man; and with the clicking of the lock and the clanging of the door, the jail population has just risen 20%. The guy lumbers back to my cell and crashes onto the empty 'bed'. The snoring begins immediately.

And the day passes on in the idleness of a classic jail cell. There just aren't a lot of perks to being in the county jail; even prison would have more benefits, the disadvantage of a longer stay notwithstanding. But I do have a lot of time on my hands; time to think about Jesus and His grace, about my family, and about all my friends and the love that binds us to one another. I've got time to kill.

Hanging out in my cell is no longer a good option, because the slumbering man on the top bunk is quite smelly. I sure hope he awakens soon and takes a shower. I don't know what's up with this guy.

God is on my mind as the hours slide away. I want food to eat. I want it now. But I think I'll wait till tomorrow to eat, so I need to keep my mind off it. The mysteries of the things of God are enough to keep my mind busy and awed, so I dig into Scripture and try to open my heart to God.

And the night passes away and I lie on my cot and sleep comfortably. The guys drone on. I awake to a new day and a new hope, a hope for some food and maybe for some letters in the near future. What a luxury that would be: connection with the outside.

The six o'clock breakfast is pretty good in the morning, perhaps because I'm really hungry. I eat and go back to bed for a while. The large man is still in the cot above me, snoring loudly. I sure hope he wakes and uses the shower in the near future. But it smells nasty in here anyway so he just kinda blends in. Come midmorning I amble out of the cell into the big room and chat with the guys and watch the morning news reruns.

About noon the deputy shows up and one of the young guys gets his ticket out of here. He's not free however; prison is his next stop. The system flexes her muscles and the people move.

And the man snores on into the afternoon and I stay out of my cell. One of the guys offers me the extra cot in his room if I want to get away from the new man. This is an offer I can not refuse and I move my stuff over. I get set up and wait for mail and I think about all my friends on the outside. And I feel sorry for myself for a while. It feels good for a bit but then it gets old and I abandon the effort. There is no mail.

But I have a Bible, so I read and pray and focus on God.

Night falls and the food arrives and we pick at it for a while and we sit around and watch the tube and talk. Darkness hovers around us and the night speeds by. Time always seems to go faster at night. At midnight I fall into my new cot and think about my family and God. I fall asleep with a picture before my eyes of a large envelope with my address on it.

And in the next cell the new guy snores away.

The sun rises to another day and the routines are followed here in the county jail. The *man* finally comes out of his deep sleep and gets cleaned up. He is pleasant enough and sits with us and chats. The inevitable question arises, "What are you in here for?"

Dear reader, do you care to guess?

Indeed, it is drugs. Possession of meth. He was just a user that got busted by the police, acting on a tip. He'd been high for a while and was all strung out when he got in here, thus the great amount of sleep.

Mid afternoon and the ole' jailor comes 'a stepping back to the room. He's got mail for me, letters from the outside. He hands me two letters and I hold the precious cargo. It's a letter from home and one from the home folks in Indiana. I hold them in my hand and simply look at them for a bit. I haven't even read them yet but they mean SO much. I don't have to tear them open for the jailor has already done that and checked the envelopes for illegal objects and codes. So I just remove the letter and read and feel the love, and shed a few tears. The letters help me a lot. Also, I get to go to work tomorrow with John, leaving at eight o'clock and returning at six. I can

The Odyssey of a Heart

hardly remember what the outside looks like, nor can I recall how it feels. All I know is how this damp, smelly cage makes me feel and what it does to me. I have been in here for a week without leaving once.

I sleep, and in the morning I eat my breakfast and prepare for a grand day outside the bars of the county jail. John shows his face at eight o'clock sharp and the jailor unlocks the door and I am free to go, for the day. Into the storage room I go and shed the orange clothes and don my civilian garb. And I walk out the door into the sunshine, right out into the open! Fresh cold air teases my face and the sky floats blue up high. Ah, the glory. Why did I never notice how great it is to be outside? We climb into the truck and drop by Casey's General Store. And I have the freedom to walk into the station and pour myself a cup of coffee and purchase it. Aren't the little things those that make freedom great?

And we drive down country roads to the jobsite, a new pole barn. The day passes with the flexing of muscles and shouting and laughing. I am DOING something. I actually enjoy working! I enter my cell at six in the evening with a satisfied feeling in my bones, and tell the guys about my day outside. None of them have the privilege of leaving this hole, but they show an interest nonetheless.

So a pattern gets laid down. I go to work on weekdays and enjoy my time outside the confining routine of the county jail. The weekend is a time for idleness and reading the many letters that flow in daily. And it's always time for reading of Scripture and prayer and meditation. The pastor and his wife show up on

The Odyssey of a Heart

Sunday mornings and give encouragement and sing a few songs. Because my father is a minister he gets to visit me one Sunday along with the Bishop from the old home church where I grew up. Everyone in here enjoys the visit.

Thanksgiving Day approaches and the prisoners have got the blues because we've got to sit in jail with lousy food to eat while most of the world gets to hang out with family and friends and eat huge amounts of food. Luckily I may go to work on holidays, too. I spend Thanksgiving out at my folk's house, working on consuming a large meal. In the evening I enter the jail room to a sight that could only come from a movie. The picnic table is entirely covered with every conceivable aspect of a classic Thanksgiving meal. The inmates are sitting around, unmoving, with a look of pleasure and pain on their faces.

I am shocked. "What in the world is going on?" I holler.

"It's the preacher," they say. "He got the church ladies to fix food for us. They went all out."

Well, aint that the truth. The variety is staggering. There is ham and turkey and stuffing; there are taters and corn and beans and bread, and there is pie and cake and candy and soda. It is WILD.

We stuff ourselves for days.

And the imprisonment of my body becomes the new normal for me. It's just the way it is. The thought of freedom twenty four hours a day sometimes teases my mind with tantalizing warmth. Someday...

In my idle time, deep thoughts roll around in my head. My body is imprisoned much like my heart had been. Unable to get beyond the negative forces in my life, I did what pleased me at the moment. Eventually this led me to drugs and into their world. Though happy most of the time, I experienced times of severe isolation and misery. Then I allowed Jesus to come into my heart and set up house. He opened the prison doors and allowed my spirit to soar free. Now my body is locked in the basement of an old courthouse, but I am not miserable.

The days pass and the date of my release arrives. I won't be released till eleven, so I go to work in the morning. We just kinda hang out and enjoy the glorious day of release. At eleven John drives back to the county jail and I amble back to my cell to gather my meager possessions. The guys are glad for me and wish me the best. I sure don't envy them right now. In the sheriff's office I finish the paperwork and collect my valuables, and show the deputy an envelope with my address on it, "**Freedom,** Indiana." He sees some humor in this, albeit decidedly less than I do.

And then I'm free and I'm on the outside, driving down the road. Unbelievable. I feel like I could do anything. I'm free!!

I take a few days to get back to Indiana. I don't want to return to work structure too quickly; right now I just want to **be,** I want to be free. I'm not as free as most people, but I'm happy for what I have. I will be on restricted probation for a long time, what this involves I am not sure, but I will have to answer to the law for what I do.

The Odyssey of a Heart

My experience at the Pentecostal church is about nine months in the past when I get out of jail. The individual saving power of Jesus I understand, it's what keeps me going. My relationship with Jesus keeps me from going out and getting stoned out of my mind. I've been living in a church setting for a while and applying for membership in this group I now seriously consider. I know that no church activity can ever substitute for the peace of God within me, but it is still a necessary step.

And it feels right to allow myself to be grafted into a body of believers. Sure the church folks aren't perfect or even close to it, but when I'm around them, say on a Sunday morning, a strange feeling rests in my chest, in my heart, and I realize I feel a deep love for the folks I share my joys and cares with. These are the ones I share my life with, these are the friends who have my back and pray for me. My brethren and sisters strengthen me in my battle against evil. To enter into a greater connection with them only makes sense.

Fresh out of jail and I'm happy and relieved and looking for focus. Gotta have focus, can't let my gaze wander. There are too many strong distractions waiting to seize me. Focusing on Jesus is crucial.

Chapter fifteen

My hands craft cabinets down at the shop as cold blow the winds of winter. No deer or rabbit hunting for me- I am on probation. We are still getting that all ironed out, but I know I'm not supposed to travel without permission and I may not own a firearm. The community service has not yet begun.

But I do a bit of traveling. A man's gotta be normal, right? The family is on top of the destination list, so I travel there. And I'm happy to be within the church at Worthington, but I also want to visit some other groups in our fellowship. One weekend in January I travel out to Ohio with some youth to visit a small church group we associate with. It promises to be a good time.

We cruise east on I-70 to Columbus, then north on 71 for a while and onto small country roads. It's nice out here; the country side is dotted with farms and large barns and silos, and the buggies rattle down the road. The bare rolling hills of midwinter are pleasing to gaze upon, the ponds are frozen, and there's snow on the ground. But down in the valleys the wind blows gently, stripped of her hilltop power.

Saturday evening dinner is at a friend of a friend's house. I walk in and am introduced to the family. The presence of one girl jolts my mind with the classic knock me off my feet routine. "Easy, easy, what's all this?" I ask myself. In a heartbeat I am strongly attracted to a total stranger.

So I'm in the area for the weekend. The youth go skating; everyone gathers for church on Sunday. The afternoon is filled with visiting and sharing spiritual insights. Somehow I remain keenly aware of this lady I have met. I definitely want to know more about her.

I travel home with my head filled with numerous thoughts, spiritually refreshed. In the following days I think much about *her*, of the possibilities. To test the attraction, I give it full opportunity to fade away.

The process of joining church continues. Each Sunday the ministers explain the Anabaptist articles of faith to us applicants. They speak of the seriousness of living in God's kingdom. The spirit of God is at work; pulsing, moving, alive.

As baptism approaches, I deal with other factors of my reality. An inspiration to become a school teacher plays in my mind, growing stronger with the passing of time. I volunteer for the job and am hired after some deliberation. You might think this process strange if you are unfamiliar with the Amish school system. The students are educated only through eighth grade; thereby it is possible for any competent adult to teach, even without training, if he or she possesses a desire to teach and a love for children. The lack of training fuels a high turnover rate, with many teachers not passing the five year mark in the profession. And this is ok; the majority of teachers are women, many who teach short term before marrying and creating a home of their own.

So, I will soon be a teacher of students. Scary thought, that is: I'm left wanting in the area of mental and spiritual strength. "Lord, I need power, in need fortitude," I pray. I haven't taught school before, but detect it might be a rather involved profession.

On March 24, 2002, I receive baptism along with three other youth. A number of folks show up, from far and near. God visits us with his presence as we follow his commandment of water baptism. Heaven rejoices as God's kingdom is symbolically strengthened.

This event is important, but perhaps not as much so as giving my heart to God. It is a blessing nonetheless. The massive support from family and friends strengthens my spirit.

Spring turns to summer and I prepare for the rigors of teaching, anticipating working with children and engaging my intellect with studies. I am moving forward, feeling more needed and rooted than I have in years. My growing attraction to the girl fuels my hope for the future. I finally attain the willingness to accept whatever the outcome might be of the hopes I hold dear. I want God's will, be it with her or without.

And the school term marches ever closer, staring at me with the weight of books unstudied and incidents unknown. It is close and alive and frightening. It demands focus and order. And to gain greater focus in my mind I must cross the line of the unknown with this stranger that I am attracted to. I need a yea or a nay from the lady. I make a few phone calls over a dry throat and a pounding heart, cutting through diplomatic layers until we finally speak one on one. She says yes!

A few weeks later she comes to visit and I see her for the second time ever. I'm usually pretty cool and collected, as my friends can testify. This however proves a bit nerve wracking. But we meet and it's great and we hang out over the weekend. What can I say? New love defies definition. If you've been in love I need tell you no more and if you haven't then you must wait and see for yourself. Suffice to say I am very happy and a bit dazed by the wonders that surround me. The day after she leaves, I swing open the doors of school for my students, and the epic adventure begins.

I now stand at a crucial crossroad. I am dating, set to enter the unknown waters of a serious relationship. Oh the lofty thoughts of love! Who can know them? My heart has been buffeted by years of pain and self destruction. As a result I built a sturdy fortress around it. Will I be able to just let go and allow the walls to fall to pieces on the ground?

****

The Odyssey of a Heart

My life in Worthington has blessings as well as challenges. The fellowship is great. Sundays I hear the Word of God concisely delivered. The spiritual war within is real, and church provides arsenal to fight the next week's battles. I am fresh off a stark, black and white encounter of Good and evil. The impossible happened as my soul was lifted from a bottomless pit. My faith is spontaneous, lively, and strong. Anything's possible. "If the Bible says it can happen, it can happen."

Unfortunately it is tough to connect with the brethren about how I feel spiritually. There is a connection, but at another level. When I sit and try to explain how REAL this all is to me, when I try to convey the joy of my newfound faith; I often feel downplayed. "Good and evil are at war, even right here. By faith in God we may experience the Good. This is HAPPENING." These things I see plainly.

I just had a close encounter with grace and that's mostly what I think about. I know that God works in the human heart if He is allowed to do so. Meanwhile my brethren think more on the practical applications of God's spirit in the church setting, a thing I am unfamiliar with.

The switch to church life is hard. It's been a long time since I have followed any pattern of order or yielding to authority. I made a mess of my life. A big mess. At my very worst, the Lord came to me and forgave all my sins. He gave me a clean slate. Nothing I did myself, other than accepting his grace, brought about a change. God gave me a gift I do not deserve.

Now I am required to give allegiance to a group of people. Misconceptions from early life rise from the grave and sit on the fringes of my mind. I fight the idea that living a morally acceptable life is what gets me right with God. I am expected to lead a good Christian life, and do so with joy. But one theme, one message, stands supreme: God forgives those who are willing to admit sin and ask for mercy. The forgiveness is complete. Most shocking of all, I can do NOTHING to earn the grace of forgiveness! I can only accept it, and then try to use it to live in a way that pleases the One who has forgiven me.

So in the mixture of raw grace and church life, I struggle to adjust. Forgiveness requires only a contrite heart; church life requires a standard of living. As I blend the two into one, the value of the brethren emerges. They are there for me. They have good advice along with their prayers. But the intimate workings of the heart are between God and me. God has come. I can not put it into words. I try but fail. So God and I share the secret of the joy within my heart. Just my Lord and I.

And the urgency of school hangs about. The classroom becomes my second home. The immensity of the task attacks me. The first days of the term saw a confused teacher attempting classes, grabbing at straws. Things go better now. My mind labors through each waking hour and I still feel inadequate. God's help is a must.

But time speeds in the classroom; things continue happening for the better. And my girlfriend and I draw closer together. Visits, phone calls, and letters

The Odyssey of a Heart

keep us in touch. We both feel God's leading. We are confident that we are on the right track. I try my best to open my heart to her, for communication is a vital element of any successful relationship, I know.

Things cruise along. We visit my folks for Christmas. Meet the parents... all goes well.

I am busy, very busy. School, church life, and courting keep me maxed out. My heart and emotions need attention as well. Unresolved pain still simmers inside. My void is filled with the soothing power of God's peace; however, areas of my life have not been exposed to its healing power. I think maybe my mental and spiritual wounds affect my dealings with other people. My heart works overtime to assure that no one can cause it pain. But life hammers away and I have little time for myself.

About six months into the courtship, doubts launch occasional attacks. I love this woman. I want to spend my life with her. But short moments of uneasiness commence to plague me. Not often at first. But after several months I deal with spots of resentment. I have allowed this person closer to my heart than anyone has been for a long time. It's scary. I withdraw, just a tad.

Now I have trouble trusting her; she has trouble trusting me. Such has become the nature of our courtship.

By this time the school board has a contract for another year of teaching. Will I sign on? I am torn. I want to, but I don't know where my life is heading. Will I be taking the *step* soon, making the big commitment? I don't know. Doubts still peck at the relationship, though I think we'll work it out.

I decide to teach again.

Chapter sixteen

The book of my life lies with blank pages open to the actions of my designation; a small portion inside the front cover is filled with history but the majority of the scroll stares at me with a clean white substance. Decisions I make with my limited knowledge and vision determine the continuation of the record. Impossible is it for me to visualize the finished product. The whole of the record of life is a grand and majestic thing indeed. But I can't see far so I forge ahead, a squint to my eyes.

One year of school teaching is completed. Oh the blessed release of pressure! The first few days after the school picnic I do nothing. Simply nothing. I am not pressured, I have no schedule. I don't have to be organized; nothing. It is great: drinking coffee, reading books, debating.

But I'm still pretty focused. Brotherhood support surrounds me. I am in the midst of a serious courtship. The school children look up to me.

I love Sundays especially. The services are the point of gathering, but there's so much more. Children are all around. I love them all dearly. Time spent with them is actually a greater joy than hanging with my peers or chatting it up with the adults. The love, the connection we feel, provides a staple of reality to my life.

The long hand of the past reaches forth to mess with the present. By now I've been on restricted probation for a year and a half, and still have some community service to perform. Traveling is complicated due to ill kept probation records. But it's not so bad. I can adjust.

My faith grows through the early stages. I believe God has a specific leading for me; a certain place for me to be, a certain thing for me to do. His will is singular. This is proven to me by the courtship, for example. After meeting a lady and having not as much as one exclusive conversation with her, I ask her out six months later, not having seen her even once in that time span. Together we feel God's leading now. It is all very clear. Such thinking is orderly and solid. It keeps the mind from confusion.

Young and in love... what an ageless theme. All is well when young love is about. Especially if the couple seeks God's will together. I marvel at the speed my life has changed. Just over two years ago I was a drug smoking drifter speeding my life down a dead end road. Then the power of God blazed through and shocked me awake. With my heart renewed, everything changed. Now children surround me. The church needs me. I am dating a godly woman.

The Odyssey of a Heart

As I mentioned earlier, the courtship hints of trouble, despite the leading from God and the love we feel for one another. Here and there a few hours of doubt interrupt the assurance that we will stay together for good. I handle these moments. I pray that our trust might grow stronger. I search for more faith. My heart is committed to climb whatever mountain and to sail whatever sea it takes for our hearts to bond stronger.

God's presence in my heart prompts my willingness to go to great lengths to seek His leading. With the doubts plaguing my mind more frequently, I decide to take things to the next level. After searching Scripture I elect to fast for seven days. This looks like a daunting race to run, but I prepare for it nonetheless. I want to know the mind of God.

On May 19, 2003, I awake from a deep slumber. I am not called for breakfast. I will consume only water for seven days.

The first impression I receive is a need for humility before God. These next days are His. It is His time to glorify HIMSELF. There is nothing I can do to help Him. I can only present Him with my humble heart.

I perceive that if my lady and I are to move back to stable ground, God Himself will need to be heavily involved.

Energy fades as day two dawns. Yesterday thoughts of food dogged me constantly, causing my chest and stomach to growl with a greater hollow than they actually contained. I tried to soak it out with water. Now the cravings return with ferocity. To distract myself I try to freshen up with a shower.

The forenoon ticks by as I study scripture and pray. I sense God's desire to move, to work. For me to pray is essential; it is my connection to the other side, to God. Inside my heart something awakens and stirs. I'm not working or doing the normal daily things. I seek God exclusively; consequently, communion with heaven switches to a far deeper level.

My very mind simplifies. With childlike eagerness I anticipate the Youth Bible Study scheduled for this evening. How exciting! A round table discussion about God. Being immersed in thoughts and writings about God, I welcome this activity.

Several truths shine into my heart as I sit with the youth and a few ministers... God gives grace to the humble. Further, if I receive grace; that means God is working within me. He desires for me to have a broken and a contrite heart before Him. Such a heart is receptive to the workings of the Spirit. And according to first Peter 5:7, I can cast all my cares upon Jesus, because he cares for me.

I want to feel like the Psalmist felt, "I delight to do Thy will, O my God: yea, Thy law is within my heart."

At home after the Bible Study, I want to eat. I want to eat SO badly. The desire is a physical thing within my body. I deny it. It is hard, hard.

Two days of focus transfer some confidence into day three. The cravings lack the acute edge of yesterday, but they aren't going anywhere just yet. It feels like they'll stick around real close today.

A new theme emerges on this bright and sunny forenoon in southern Indiana. Industrial and domestic life swirls around me as I occupy a bubble of absorption. I crave food. It takes on a magical, almost mythical proportion. My flesh wants to dwell thereon constantly. If I allow it to, I feel despondent and weak. It is hard to keep fighting.

Turning wholly to God is the solution. Throwing myself onto the will of God takes my focus off all else. The workings of Jesus are the only sane place to rest my mind upon. It is either follow my base desire to eat, or immerse myself in the spirit of God. Nothing else really exists. Just these two factors.

Time marches on. I sleep. I wake to another day, day four. Discomfort rolls through body as breakfast then break time pass by. Me, I stay in my room with the ever present glass of water close at hand. A search into scripture yields yet another gem. I realize I can't always depend on my earthly knowledge and reasoning in the making of big decisions, such as courtship stuff. Some ideas I harbor require no faith to stay alive. But I see now that perhaps God can provide a view or leading that I wouldn't find myself. I must be able to believe that God can grant me the wisdom I need.

In the afternoon a sharp pain jabs me on my left side. My chest tightens and my stomach shoots darts inward. Simply walking takes energy rapidly. Ironically, I enjoy moments of near euphoria.

I feel called to simply have faith in God's leading.

My body howls with the anguish upon awakening on day five. Little strength remains in my system and physical weakness drags on my mind as well. I feel vulnerable to the advances of the evil one. The urgency of need presses on me. The reader will recall I am living in a world of only two forces. It is either concentrate on God or slip into despondency. And now I feel too weak to even direct my mind to God. As I struggle for help, a vision forms in my mind. I see God's hand, large and strong. I am being held in the safety of the palm. It is real! God supports me.

Strength flows into my heart.

Reading in Isaiah, a theme catches my attention. Repeatedly the words "I am the Lord" appear. They roll over and over in my mind. I begin to understand a bit more of God's sovereignty. He is the Creator. He is above all. He is the power of goodness in my life. I can listen to Him and follow His direction, for I am certainly not the guy in control. My heavenly Father is.

It seems I need to suffocate my doubts about the relationship with my girlfriend and commit myself to staying the course. I feel that God intends that we be together; therefore, I need to open my heart as I search His leading.

So I hack at the wall enclosing my heart.

The sixth day falls on Sunday, and on this day I am on a higher plane. I feel great as I walk to Church at the neighbors house. My mind is clear. Love floods my heart as I stand among the brethren. I almost picture Jesus in our midst, blessing the gathering.

Afterwards I meander back to the house. Longings for food again plague my mind as my heart struggles to stay open to God's spirit. Despondency knocks hard at the door.

The Odyssey of a Heart

Oh the urgency to live in the immediacy of God's Word! Feeling a need for divine leading, I research some references on 'lead'. I gain a sense of being led, and a deep peace returns.

Any thoughts on the girlfriend, you wonder. Actually, I think on that a lot. The desire to plunge my heart right on in only increases. I think I see direction and some stability. I want to draw closer.

And then the anticipated, the prized day seven. By now my outlook has been reduced to an unsophisticated, childlike joy. Just being alive thrills me. I am reduced before a holy God. Going into the fast I had my own agenda. Well, the Lord took over swiftly. I perceived right away that things were going to happen on God's time and in His way. Humbling, it was.

Physical weakness pervades within, but it is only secondary. Toward evening I break the fast with some orange juice. WOW! Never before have I known such richness of flavor. Amazingly, I feel immediate strength.

Later I speak with *her* on the phone. We rejoice for the friendship we share. God is moving, working, and I feel confident that He will help us to work out our differences and grow stronger in love and trust, to grow in the things that really matter.

Tired and happy, I fall asleep knowing that I need even more self control now that I've started eating again. I need to not go and gouge myself like I want to. The past week feels huge and strange and epic; it feels almost unbelievable. For seven days my heart and mind fought the desire of my flesh and struggled to stay focused on the Lord alone. Seven days ticked away, sometimes slow and sometimes with timeless swiftness. With God's help I'd endured.

In this thing of fasting rests a deep truth. I don't understand it deeply so I can't explain it well. But I started out with a plan in mind. I desired to seek God. Once begun, the fast quickly became the Lord's. He took over and gently showed me the terms to be followed. The terms, the conditions for my heart could only be fulfilled with His help. Then moving on in I perceived I would have to be willing to follow God's direction, no matter what it might be. That was hard to do. But God helped me lay my ideas, plans, and desires on the altar of Christian life.

I have changed. My abilities of description present poor means to show how it is. It is different. God is in control. Everywhere.

I feel as a child might, walking across a meadow with daddy, hand in hand.

I go to see my girlfriend. Life feels great. All is well.

I am confident that ground breaking new heights will be reached on the visit. Has not God instructed me to open up my heart and to dig in for the long haul? Have I not laid my all on the altar? How could it not work?

My friend, I learn a thing or two about confusion, anger, and a sense of helplessness over the next days. The issues at hand are only more complicated; we are miles farther apart than ever before. There is little trust, from me or from her. We talk, our opposition to each other's views slamming down a granite

The Odyssey of a Heart

wall between us, cutting off the possibility of real communication. I am angry and confused.

My heart tells me it will never work. I push the thought away.

I go home with confusion on my mind, recalling our resolves to be more open. We both know there is a big problem and we both feel the other one is it; but we skirt the obvious and forge ahead. And I simply don't understand what is going on. I thought God had provided a clear leading, now I wonder if I've even glimpsed a shadow of His intentions. Scary thing is, I promised to follow His leading no matter what.

Over the next month our trust steadily declines and love struggles to stay warm. Unresolved issues simmer. I suffer attacks of GET OUT! OUT! OUT! I reason and force these away. If the relationship doesn't work out I will have to completely rethink my understanding of God's will, of the way God works. My heart resists the turmoil thereof. Besides, I love her.

The summer wears on.

Another visit looms. I teeter on the edge, desperately wanting to stay in. But getting out spells relief from a numbingly difficult situation. I feel stranded, without the leading of God. I can no longer make sense out of what He wants in this situation. Then, days before the visit I mow a graveyard on my community service ticket. The motor roars and my mind runs and my heart screams for release. For a whole day, my only desire is to get out of a painful relationship that I can neither control nor understand. On this day the relationship's death sentence is sealed, the verdict is in.

I go to see my girlfriend, the one I've been dating for a year and a day, precisely. My whole being trembles in the grip of numbness. I do what I have to do. It hurts. Very, very much. We talk, I say goodbye, I leave. I walk out at 11:30 PM. A haunted feeling savagely devours my heart as the screen door slams on dreams dashed and hopes obliterated.

Brother Reuben roars up in his black Chevrolet and we head west. He drove hundreds of miles to pick me up. He is there when I need him.

We drive all night. We talk and I grieve. I grieve for love lost, for pain inflicted, and for pain received. Circumstances whirl around me; confusion engulfs me. I don't understand God's will in this and can't even start to detect His leading. I'll just have to sit tight for a time. A long time.

Chapter seventeen

In the ensuing months I come to understand more deeply the powers of anger, bitterness, and loneliness. Having felt a strong leading going into the relationship, I now float over an abyss of confusion. What's going on anyway? What is the will of God? How am I to make decisions? Why do I have to hurt again? Have I not given my all to God? And how do I handle my heart now? Do I stay open; do I stay vulnerable?

Ah, my friend. Why would I keep my heart out in the danger zone? Why would I be vulnerable if I could instead withdraw into an isolated corner of quiet; a place that beckons and welcomes me with the warm embrace of numbness?

Far back in the shadows away from everyone I see a vacancy. I go there. Here I will sit and brood, I will think, read, and distract myself. No one will touch me here; I will NOT be hurt.

I shut down. My vision blurs. My focus wanes. I get by OK not paying attention to my heart, plugging in physically to the church but keeping my heart back. It's not too bad guarding my heart from everyone and keeping my thoughts to myself and forcing my feelings back where they came from. Hey, I'm tough, thank you. But sometimes at night when no one is around and the wind moans through the trees outside, I can't escape it and the isolation gouges and slices my soul. Deep.

And I wonder, what's up with this? The recent past has seen me rise scarred and bleeding but ultimately joyful from the sinkhole of drug use, leave life as I knew it behind and join myself with a tight knit brotherhood community, and commence teaching school and dating a Godly woman. Have I not seen enough confusion? Why is so much of my life bordering on depression? Did I do something wrong or isn't the Christian on easy street after all? Where has all the joy gone?

In this dark hour of despair family quietly lends her support to my otherwise wandering spirit. A bond of love wraps her arms around my fragile frame; the security is just plain THERE. Family. The concern of my parents hovers over me; the silent yet powerful love of my brothers feeds strength to my soul; and my sisters offer their affection. The ancient bond of family connections lends her rock solid surety as my heart weathers the hurricane of circumstances.

Brother David and his new bride Barbara live next door in a small cabin, bravely starting out into the thing called marriage. I love hanging out in the comfortable setting of their home, drinking strong coffee and discussing books, ideas, religion; you name it. They see life as it is; they are genuine and practical people.

One lazy Saturday David and I trade memories of bygone days, especially our teen years in Iowa. We enjoy reminiscing about the hunting and hockey games and youth gatherings and the characters that made up our home church. Excessive caffeine makes it all seem more glorious still. Ah, the great days of old…

"You know what," I say, "I could go back home for a while and live with the family." The thought hits me abruptly. What an idea. Back home to the family, back home into my past. Suddenly I'm excited.

So we discuss this idea for a while. Being with my family, just being there, may well give me the focus I so greatly lack now. You know, I could actually do this. All the glory of the good I could experience, of the atonement for the past, dances around me and excites my senses.

Directly I plunge into battle. I want to go. I could go. But I've had the possibility ruled out for some time now. Go back home and face the community again? Try to break through the barriers that my violent actions of yester year have created? Jump into a different church fellowship? Move back under my father's roof? Obstacles indeed.

But I want to go.

The joys I feel from the last few years at home are over shadowed by the stress I felt and multiplied while there. It was a time of hiding, of pain, of disobedience. Leaving for good at eighteen, it was about abandoning my younger brothers and worrying

The Odyssey of a Heart

my parents sick and disappointing my sisters. It was about hardening my conscience and stuffing my anger and all my other emotions down out of sight. These memories hurt.

I could redeem at least a portion of the past.

The drain of heavy thinking exhausts me in the days following. The passion within is a magnet pulling me toward my family where I vaguely sense a redemption to be found, a payback for years wasted. My practical mind examines reality and loudly says no. Oh the confusion, the fury of battle.

School is the wild card in the hand. What is more intimately part of childhood than school? Before me I have growing children, each with his personal set of joys, desires, struggles and pain. They look to me for love and understanding, for guidance to counter the insecurities of youth. They have the questions I never asked at their age. They need answers. And I desperately want to be THERE for them.

The past reaches forth with a heavy hand to affect my decisions for the future. Despite the obstacles confronting me, I still want to move back home for a while. I want to stay for the students, but what about my little brother at home, growing up without even one brother there for him? Who matters more? A feeling that I have seriously abandoned my past hangs over me constantly. Further complicating the situation is probation. If I go I'll have to stay two and a half years at which point the law will leave me alone.

The school term moves into the second half. I must decide if I'll be in command at school next year. I know God will provide an indication only if I'm fully willing to follow the sign, no matter what it is. If I hold back I block His leading.

With great effort I lay my desires at God's feet; my will slowly yielding to His. Eventually I can only conclude I need to stay put and teach again. Why I can't be with my family I don't know, but I accept it as best I can.

****

The human heart and mind struggle for the clarity of clear direction from a higher source. Questions and confusions float throughout the consciousness. These receive but scant attention when no major decisions loom. The larger mysteries and harder questions are at times mercifully lost under the focus of daily living in one's circle of human contact. But lo, ever returning sooner or later, they surface with a demand for leading and focus. Swimming amongst a vision still remaining and a focus now wavering, the person seeks for guidance.

In such a setting I search for focus for my now isolated existence. The agony of breaking off a serious courtship serves well to grease the wheels on the carriage already bearing my heart and emotions to a lonely planet of self-sufficiency. I am by no means a constantly depressed person lacking joy and happiness. I experience the normalcy that surely serves as reality for millions daily. Something is amiss, however. My silent isolation weighs heavily into this

The Odyssey of a Heart

void. The need for help from others brings a feeling I despise. My mind and heart work in solitude.

And now I decide to stay put and quell the titanic urge within to go and be with my family. An old tendency to question God knocks at my door. I could easily believe that God is not just. In fact, I have a hard time convincing myself otherwise. Who has not blamed God for the problems of life? What is more natural for human nature than harboring unrealistic notions about the Power that can control all things?

But I can no longer think of God as being unjust. Over the past few years I couldn't shake the nagging doubt whispering to me an argument against God. Considering the host of social and family problems that befall humanity, I attempted to form an understanding that made some sense. I failed. To my mind came no logical answer for all the suffering and confusion that grips our species. That God would allow such pain to live in the hearts of men made no sense. I searched the Bible, trying to convince myself that God is just after all.

Situations beyond my control arose in my life. Emotional pain, rejection, and bitterness took their turns battering my heart. Meanwhile I pondered the problems of those around me. Then in the midst of the worst loneliness and bitterness I've known, a peace crept into my very soul. Many things made no sense and I still hurt. But I began to understand God DOES know what He's doing. I couldn't find a way to fix much, but in a strange way God's love answered the question in my soul. God is just; God is in loving control.

Now I feel but one desire: to KNOW the God who loves me.

Chapter eighteen

My journey over the past year and a half has been nothing if not full of unexpected twists and turns. Almost nothing has gone the way I had planned. I'm trying to understand if I'm merely wandering along or if the Lord is leading me in some way.

After completing my second year of teaching, I promptly headed for Iowa to spend the summer with my family. I thought Indiana probation would allow me to do so: go for a short stay without moving my residence. Unfortunately I made the mistake of traveling without first making the necessary arrangements with my probation officer. The first day I was gone I received a tense call from her, a signal that I was treading on thin ice. She duly notified Missouri of my unauthorized travels.

So there I was in Illinois with the Indiana and Missouri probation departments breathing down my neck. I had been unsure of how the visiting thing

The Odyssey of a Heart

would work, but it was quickly becoming clear that there were some major complications indeed.

I had a choice to make. I could turn around and slink back to Indiana and disappoint my family at home. They were expecting to have me there for the summer, for crying out loud. Or I could follow my heart and blaze on out to Iowa, but I'd have to move my probation there. And there was no guarantee that I wouldn't see the cold walls of a jail cell again. I had broken probation by traveling out of state without permission.

A few phone calls, some shouting and several dire threats later, all my cards lay on the table. Being caught between two states created huge confusion; nobody knew what was going on and I got the brunt of the frustration of all other parties. With the belittling voices of law officers ringing in my ears I neared a decision. Instinct was about all that remained, for it was very difficult to sort out leadings or indications or feelings. Instinct told me of my desire to be at home again. She spoke of the loss to be regained. She whispered of the joys to be had.

My mind wandered through the maze of family, church, community and law; and again to family. My family trumped all other factors. I didn't care what the church or the law did to me; I wanted to go home and simply be there for a while.

I went.

Unsettling doubts probed my brain the first days at home. The law and my church were not a little perturbed at my actions being committed without their counsel being sought. Frustrated that I couldn't

The Odyssey of a Heart

just stand on my two feet and make acceptable decisions, I merely withdrew as my friends scrutinized my character. The reverberations of distrust I hated most of all. That was deeply demoralizing.

So it was sit tight and wait out the storm and accept the results.

I felt great but I didn't. I was having a great time but I wasn't. I was a scoundrel in the eyes of the law, and quite possibly a scoundrel in the eyes of the brethren I'd forsaken in Indiana. I wasn't sure what to think; I was tied down in Iowa because of probation but left feeling I'd made a big mistake. About everyone else thought I'd made a bad choice. At home is where I wanted to be, no matter what anyone thought. But I was confused; trust in God rocked under the strain of insecurity.

It was good to be back though. Every road and farm for miles around lay etched in my mind. This was home, the place of my earliest memories. This was my land.

A month or two rolled by before I received word I'd been written up for violating probation by traveling; consequently, I must appear before the Honorable Judge of Scotland county Missouri. Now, that sent me into a tailspin. Frantically I called an attorney and agreed to his high monetary terms if he would only help me get rid of this major crisis. Indeed, I faced the very real possibility of more jail time. But the attorney didn't charge a hundred and fifty dollars an hour for nothing, so two agonizing months later the charge went away with me never setting foot inside the courtroom. I parted with a few days' wages though.

And then I was at it again in the classroom, doing duty at a school in only its second year of existence. By then the law was leaving me alone and I felt comfortable with the whole church thing. I did however have to report regularly to probation and they were nice enough to burden me with a few headaches such as restricting me to one county and imposing a ten pm curfew. I could deal with that; I didn't want to run afoul of the steely arm of the law ever again. I could feel good about myself. I was a school teacher, was I not? Are not school teachers a staple of society?

****

I am now in my second year of teaching here in Iowa. Last term sailed along more smoothly than I could comprehend. The students stayed enthused. The parents remained supportive. My sister Laura taught beside me. If teaching can be easy, it was so last year.

Resisting the strong encouragement of the entire school, I declined the teaching position for this year. Pretty hard, it was. I feel a sense of duty of sorts to school teaching. But I suffered a few long periods of disinterest at school last year and just wasn't focused enough to become willing to give it another shot.

Throughout the summer I labored in construction, earning my living by the sweat of my brow. Different school boards stopped by... "So, what are you working this fall? We need a school teacher, actually.

The Odyssey of a Heart

We thought you might be interested." I declined the offers each time. Fleeting desires to teach presented themselves at odd moments. I didn't think on them much. I wanted a year off.

The community constructed a new school this year over in my old neighborhood. Come crunch time, they still had no teachers. I kinda wanted to teach there, enough so that I almost volunteered. When the board asked the second time, I said why not.

I'm having a large time.

The four upper grade boys are a major highlight of the school term. We DO things together. The class discussions burst with the energy of ideas and imagination, some of which would be better suited for the playground. We get to swap stories of interest: travel, space, riddles, and peers. Competitive softball keeps our edge sharp. The younger students provide many memories as well. It's hard to match the youthful energy of a third grade class.

I'm doing what I love: teaching, encouraging, exhorting, debating, and guiding. I'm talking math, language, geography, and writing skills. The school house pulses with the energy of students, the power of mind and body. Each day is alive.

Were it not for one key element, I would not be receiving all these blessings. This element is crucial to who I am. My very Christian identity hangs upon it. It is a matter of the heart.

Early in my Christian life I simply lived from the heart. It came naturally. My heart was open to anyone who cared to communicate. Seared emotions healed steadily as they were exposed to the grace of God and that of my fellow men. God's Word entered and lodged in my mind and heart. Helping others became my singular focus. Deep within arose an enormous desire for others to experience the peace and healing I felt. Seeing another heart in pain sliced my soul every time. I sought to be used by God no matter what. I was willing to bear pain if others could benefit from it.

Over time events commenced pushing my heart back into isolation. I came a little too close to a few people emotionally. Old, unresolved hurts surfaced and grated against my peace. I couldn't convey to anyone how I really felt. The spiritual powers I'd experienced were so intense I couldn't connect well on that level. But the biggest blow to my heart-openness undoubtedly was delivered by the failed courtship. The post-relationship pain and confusion so indelibly stamped my heart that I feel it to this day. My view of God's nature took a heavy blow as my heart plunged into a slide I'm still recovering from, though I've curbed most of its damage.

So by this past year, my heart shut down. I existed. I went through the motions of family, church, and school. But it was all so surface level. Nothing happened down at that level where it really matters. Life did not engage my passions.

My heart had felt pain and reacted the only way it knew how: it shut down. Being shut down, it hoped to be clear of painful encounters. As you know, that never works. Isolation hurts as much as anything, just differently.

The Odyssey of a Heart

Consequently, I wasn't into teaching. I bailed. Then over the summer I spent time with a Christian counselor. Sitting and chatting, Sam the counselor and I examined my condition. This guy was good. I just naturally felt comfortable and willing to talk about the stuff I shut everyone else off from. So we talked and shared and slowly a profound clarity commenced dawning on me. I had withdrawn DEEPLY into myself, no longer anything like the open person that bubbled forth with the joy of communication the first few years after my conversion. I was shocked as I realized the very real danger my isolation had drawn me into. My spirit was weak and driven away from others.

I'd never consciously thought, "I'm shutting down." My desire wasn't to be selfish. But I had selfishly avoided pain at all cost. Relationships are risky by their very nature; they moved off limits. If others hurt, I wasn't of much help. Spiritual inspirations granted me weren't passed on. I simply evolved into a rather wooden being.

Sam and I candidly discussed all this. He called me back out into the arena of life. With scriptural truths he showed me a better way. Engage! Someone need comfort? Comfort them. Anyone need understanding? Listen. Is a relationship in your life in turmoil? Don't back out. Stay there! Stay engaged! Live from the heart. Allow God to work.

I needed to lean on God for help. I had to risk getting hurt, otherwise my heart fell short of the arena of blessing. I needed to say the things hard to say, to do the deeds hard to perform. I had to lay up treasures of the heart; treasures in heaven.

Consequently I found myself willing to invest my heart back into teaching students. Within me rose a deep longing to build meaningful relationships, to work with things eternal.

It doesn't come easy, but I strive to live from the heart. If someone hurts, I try to care. If someone's confused, I desperately want to be there for the person. I want to listen, to speak, to do, and to understand. I desire that my heart form genuine bonds with others.

The difference glares. Living on the surface and keeping the heart alone brings no peace. How well I know the emptiness of isolation! Living only out of the mind hardens and distracts the heart. Your loved ones suffer for it.

The fullness of God's love springs from a heart turned to Him. Living from the heart is difficult. The effort is well worth it, however. There is a "Peace which passeth all understanding." Living openly is the only way. There is strength of character available at the heart level.

Although the power that would draw me into isolation is consuming, I choose to stay open.

Epilogue

Memories from the short years of my life flood my mind as I sit here and write. The scope of my experience, joy and pain and everything in between, escapes the grasp of my comprehension. I've worked, played, been happy, felt joy; writhed in the grip of rage and bitterness and loneliness, despaired under the power of evil, rejoiced in the presence of God, and endured in the face of temptation. I have found God to be ever real, if not always consciously so.

A half dozen points rise up and speak to me as I review my life. They are that which I have seen from the eye of the storm: living a double life and hiding a part of oneself is destructive and holds no peace; the church needs to realize that all youth, no matter how rebellious, have good in their hearts and are in search of something genuine; a change of life MUST start in the heart; if one is utterly willing to follow God, He WILL give the power to overcome; God is an active force , an unseen reality greater than all physical things we see; the only true way to live is to live from the HEART, being willing to perform difficult communicative tasks and to open up one's heart to another person.

A double life is a quagmire by design. My early life epitomized a confused hiding. Unwilling to heed my conscience impartially, I picked and chose. Immediately the uncertainty began. For when you deny it in part, what is the balance of a healthy conscience? Hiding a part of yourself fosters an isolation of sorts; you must hide partially from most people. I must believe this affects your ability as a whole in relating to others.

I don't suggest one should have no private thoughts, ideas, or desires. Such is the God given right of each human. It's the faking, the putting up a front, which leads to inner turmoil and uncertainty.

The matter of rebellious youth in the church continues as a current and important issue. Your mind even now leaps to someone, I am sure. Unfortunately this person has chosen to defy order to some degree, be it in the home or in the church; most likely in both. This person's actions and attitude may portray a disregard and disrespect for people and their feelings and rights. There is pain being inflicted, to be certain. And you think, "Why doesn't that boy just straighten up? How can he hurt his family like that? The nerve of him. He needs to be taught a lesson. He simply will not be allowed to continue like this."

And some of those things are valid. The church can't simply sit on her heels and allow chaos to reign.

The Odyssey of a Heart

But allow me to say here, and I say it without a shred of doubt, that ALL youth contain goodness within themselves. You might not notice, but it's there.

God created man and called it good. It is important to note that the rebellious youth in question is created by God. His body, mind and soul are God's handiwork. Thus reason tells us that while these faculties operate, they do so by God's power. Sure the person might not be right with God, but there's good contained in his being. If a person had nothing good contained within him, he would be the devil incarnate.

Having then seen the youth to be not all bad, why not focus on the good within him. Let a few people hold him accountable for his actions. But even more, let the greater number focus on the good things they expect of him. Believe he wants to work righteousness. Understand the pain within him. There is always pain, you know, where there is rebellion. Treat him with respect. Play on the goodness that's in his heart.

So, a change of life for the youth is the desire of the church. And a change of life is necessary. Change can be good.

How exactly does change come about? Can someone just change at will and morph into a better person? How does one gain lasting victory over sin?

My people are a society living apart, secluded in varying degrees from the whims of American culture. We strive to be in God's commandments, residing in a close knit community. A standard of performance is expected of everyone. We are visually set apart by our plain clothes and somewhat rough haircuts. The rules and expectations stand clear.

These strong points can easily fall into a crucial weak point. Say a rebellious youth wishes to live inside the approval of God and the church. *He can quit breaking the rules and keep a low profile, and he will be accepted as a reformed individual.* And he well may be. But a danger lurks: a person may outwardly appear to be righteous, while inside his heart nothing has changed.

Because of the need for performance within the plain churches, this danger is especially strong there. It is very important to realize this. Renewing of the HEART holds the only solution for true change. "The sacrifices of God are a broken spirit: a broken and a contrite heart, O God, thou wilt not despise." From a renewed heart will flow the outward change that will lift performance to an acceptable level and beyond.

In no way do I suggest that outward evidence of change is unnecessary. Quite the opposite is true. But the whole story MUST go infinitely deeper than eyes can see. The heart empowered by God perseveres. Temptations lack their former power. Victory over sin becomes reality, though the struggle will continue.

So once again, let a few hold the youth accountable for her actions. But let the greater number look beyond the actions and ask, "What is happening in the heart?" After much thought and prayer, build a relationship with the young person. When trust is established, reach out to her heart. Oh my friend, I plead with you even as my tears fall upon this page. Many, many people desperately need a friend at the heart level, a friend to understand and help them. It is a need of the heart.

The Odyssey of a Heart

Change is a necessary element, and change is good. But the only TRUE change begins in the heart.

Come the time a person desires God above all else, victory will be had. God stands ready and waiting for the moment a heart opens wholly to Him. No barriers, no putting off till later, nothing. One needs only to reach a point holding no separation from this awesome and mysterious, yet incomprehensibly intimate and immediate Spirit. Reach an arena of the present moment, and the heart trembles.

And God gives power and victory and peace. Simply denying oneself all lame excuses and procrastinations opens the flood gates to a whole new power. But it must be in the RIGHT NOW. Don't push it off for a month, three weeks, two days or even one hour. Surrender to God RIGHT now. God lives in the present moment; He will be found nowhere else. Only after the heart and mind gather their wanderings from the past and the future can God help in the present. Only in such a setting is true help available.

God will help. But you MUST desire His help and acceptance above all things. ALL THINGS.

Nothing can match the peace of complete surrender.

The person that chooses to surrender his heart to God in the immediacy of the moment of conviction will discover a God beyond comprehension. Sure God is real. But have you ever sensed His presence so strongly that the very air around you pressed inward? Has God ever manifested Himself so clearly that you felt as if His divine nature soaked right through your mind?

The Odyssey of a Heart

You have lived for a time here on planet earth. Your memory serves you an assortment of happenings and experiences you have seen, felt and done. Underscoring these memories, for those with physical vision, are the things seen. You know you walk on the ground because you see it. You vision provides evidence of the reality of the objects around you.

God is invisible, but real nonetheless. If and when He chooses to manifest Himself even slightly, the evidence of His reality far surpasses the evidence of things seen. God is alive, happening, encompassing. He reigns active, personal, supreme.

I search for more words, but in vain. Were there words to do justice in describing God, my mind couldn't grasp or contain them anyway.

How should we then live, having such a great and active power of mercy around and within us? How to truly live a life of worth and meaning?

Living from the heart is the answer. How to live from the heart is too great a subject to cover here. But suffice to say that most of you can discern between closing off the heart as opposed to opening it up to care, to understand, to rejoice, and to sorrow.

Living from the heart is hard. It is hard to tell someone how you really feel. It is hard to admit to yourself that you need help. It is hard to care when the waves of personal, family, and social crises wash over you.

But keeping your heart in the battle is the only way to win.